TITANIC
LESSONS

Do Historic Realities Predict
Problems for a Growing Church?

Hollis L. Green,
ThD, PhD

GlobalEdAdvance
Press

TITANIC LESSONS

Do historic realities predict problems for a growing Church?

Copyright © 2008, 2012 by Hollis L. Green

Library of Congress Control Number: 2012940678

TITANIC LESSONS

ISBN 978-0-9796019-6-5

Subject Codes and Description: 1. REL108010 Religion: Christian Church - Growth   2. REL014000 Religion: Christian Church - Church Administation 3. REL016000 Religion: Institutions & Organizations

Cover Design by Barton Green

Printed in Australia, Brazil, France, Germany, Italy, Spain, UK, and USA.

The Press does not have ownership of the contents of a book; this is the author's work and the author owns the copyright. All theory, concepts, constructs, and perspectives are those of the author and not necessarily the Press. They are presented for open and free discussion of the issues involved. All comments and feedback should be directed to the Email: [*comments4author@aol.com*] and the comments will be forwarded to the author for response.

Published by

GlobalEdAdvance Press

www.gea-books.com

This edition, published on the 100th anniversary of the Titanic disaster, is dedicated to

Those who willingly gave their lives to save other passengers on the Titanic.

and

To those faithful pastors who personally struggle daily to minister to needy individuals in their community.

Table of Contents

Author's Preface

My fifty-year attempt to support Christianity at the congregational level required a generic blindness to the sectarian nature of American Christianity. This journey provided a less biased framework for social research related to the barriers caused by the clustering of churches into sectarian denominations. The effort to understand the church as a social institution and develop an appreciation for my religious heritage enhanced my personal Christian life and provided a basis for continued research, but brought concern related to the unholy desire to grow until a particular church is the largest in the geographic area.

Knowing that there were limitations to all growth, the mystery became how large could a gathered church grow until the natural limitations and detrimental forces begin to operate against the watch-care of the people. Would paid staff with specific job descriptions replace the heart and soul of pastoral ministry? Would individual needs get the same attention they had received in the church where family and friends were present?

Another concern was how large can such a program become until it ceases to be a true church with adequate watch-care for all the people. Would such a large groupbecome either a club for saints, or a kind of Super-Mart of religion? Would such unnatural growth bring about the disintegration of small community churches served by hardworking and caring men with the assistance of unpaid lay leadership who performed sufficient watch-care over the congregation and the community? Would this effective instrument of community life and service to families become redundant as members flocked to be lost in the crowd of some super-church? These questions have not been answered, but some observations, assumptions, and conclusions have initiated the writing of this book.

SEARCH FOR ANTECEDENT CAUSES

My search for antecedent causes for Protestant divisions has taken me into every region of the United States and required extensive travel in twenty-six countries, Research was directed toward the social and cultural foundations of Protestant denominations. The problem of negative participation in the worship and educationalprograms of small community congregations has created declining attendance, as well as thedestructive aspects of personal mental reservation to commitment and a cognitive dissent to the basic doctrines of Christianity.

In an effort to understand the sectarian view, extensive research was done on the oldest American Pentecostal denomination and the largest American Protestant group. Doctorates in Theology and in Philosophy were earned during this search. Meanwhile, my schedule was filled with academic research and writing, but colleagues and friends have encouraged sequels to my best known works in this genre; Why Churches Die ISBN 978-0-9796019-0-3 and Why Christianity Fails in America ISBN 978-0-9796019-1-0. This volume, Titanic Lessons, is a follow-up to those two books related to church growth.

— Hollis L. Green, ThD, PhD

ORDER OTHER BOOKS BY THIS AUTHOR FROM:

GLOBALEDADVANCEPRESS

www.gea-books.com

CHAPTER ONE

Somber Warning from Untrustworthy Patterns

CAUTION IN COPYING PROGRAMS, PLANS AND POLICIES

This incident happened to me in Oxford, England in the early 1960's. After spending a considerable amount of time in the "religion" section of a large used bookstore, seven (7) books were selected. Presenting them to the gray haired gentleman at the counter, his comments were both surprising and shocking. He asked, "Are you an American?" My answer was in the affirmative. He then asked, "Are you a member of the cloth?" Declaring myself a member of the clergy, the old gentleman pleaded, "Please don't take these books to America. They have already emptied the churches in England!" Out of respect to his wisdom and sincerity, the books were left on the counter.

Walking out into the cold air of reality, it was disturbing to contemplate the reality that American clergy and churches were reading books and following old thinking patterns from England and

Germany that had proved untrustworthy. I was grateful for the lesson learned from the English gentlemen that gave insight and caution about picking anything out of another language, culture, or time period and expecting it to work adequately in the local church.   Christian leaders in different regions of the United States and particularly those outside the USA should take caution in copying the programs, plans and policies of other churches. It is a fact that when one translates words, concepts, or ideas from one language or culture to another, the meaning changes.

Scriptural principles have not changed, but each national culture must be careful to present the Gospel in the language and social context of the community they wish to reach. If the Day of Pentecost taught the church anything, it is clear that individuals should not have to cross cultural and/or language barriers to hear the Good News in the language of their birth. The character and social fabric of each culture and society is complicated and Christianity must work diligently to communicate the gospel in a frame of reference and in terms easily understood in the context of each culture and language. This is why the pluralistic mix in a Growing Church predicts certain problems that have not been adequately addressed. This work will deal with a few, but there will still be unanswered questions.

WALLS CANNOT PROTECT

Walls did not protect the Empire of China and buildings of brick and mortar will not protect Christianity from the onslaughts of New Age thinking, liberal theology, or an ego-centered ministry. A Wall is no stronger than the Keeper at the gate. A theology or philosophy is no stronger than those who teach and practice the discipline. No investment of money, men, and material is sufficient to protect individuals or institutions from outside forces when the priest of the family, the teachers in faith-based institutions, or the keeper of the gate can be distracted or disarmed. There must be a strategy to protect those principles and values that are sacred in a moral society. Walls cannot protect a society from the enemy within or without.

Keepers of the Gates along the Wall

When Robert C. Byrd was the Junior Senator from West Virginia, he spoke at a meeting of a service club. He had committed to memory the details about the Great Wall of China. The wall was 4,160 miles across Northern China. It was a structure large enough to be seen from the moon with the naked eye. Wall construction started as far back as Chinese recorded history. Prisoners of war, convicts, soldiers, civilians and farmers provided the labor. Millions died for this cause, and many Chinese stories speak of parted lovers and men dying of starvation and disease. Materials used for the wall were whatever could be found near by: clay, stone, willow branches, reeds and sand. Thousands of bodies have been discovered buried in the foundations of the wall, or used to make up its thickness.

The audience listened closely as Senator Byrd told of the years it took to build the wall and the cost of material and lives. Particularly, how workers who died on the job were entombed in the wall. The wall was built to keep China's enemies from attacking or conquering sections of the country. History reveals that the wall worked well when the country was strong. Only when a dynasty was weakened from within, were invaders from the north able to advance and conquer. In the many years since the wall was completed, not a single invader ever breached the wall. They did not have to scale the wall or break it down; they simply bribed the keepers of the gates. In reality, no wall of protection is stronger than the individuals and the institutions that guard the gates. The question is not, where is a church that is large enough to protect the Nation; the appropriate question is, where are the men to stand in the gap and guard the gates to the family and the homes of America?

ONE-ROOM SCHOOL VS. PRESENT SECONDARY SYSTEM

America had an excellent grammar school system for many years. It worked and generated the men and women that led America through a civil war, economic depression, two world wars created a super power with the best economy in the world. Remember all these leaders were prepared under the old system. Change began about 1915 and accelerated until the early 1960's when America decided to copy the failed system of Russia and eliminate prayer, and values education from the classroom. This could not or would not have happened without the abandonment of the one-room, community based, family friendly, grammar school.

When America abandoned the one-room community based grammar school, what was gained? It would be good to take a look at the present elementary/secondary education in light of what precipitated the change and why it was so necessary to place the government in control of elementary/ secondary education. Search the travel records of the early leaders of the NEA and see how many trips were made overseas to study the educational system of the USSR. Then and only then will some of the changes become clear, but the damage is already done. Look at what we had and ask the basic question: are we better off now?

In the one-room school, grades 1-8 met together. One teacher taught all students in all grades in one room. The older children were able and willing to assist the teacher with the needs of the younger students. A child having a hard time with fourth grade math was able to listen again to the third grade lesson and gain a better understanding. A student advanced in fifth grade math could hear the lesson given to the sixth graders and be challenged to grow. The day of small things should never be despised.   The one-room school did a good job because it was small, intimate, attentive to the needs of individuals, controlled by the community, and had family support. These dynamics were lost when the one-room school was abandoned. All the king's horses and all the kings men with all the king's wealth cannot put the scrambled educational process together again. Big is not necessarily better!

COMPARISON OF OUTCOMES

Many educators look back to those days of achievement and are troubled by the comparison of outcomes with the present system. In an enlightened and affluent Nation where there are as many functionally illiterates as there are college graduates; something in education is not better! Bigger classes in larger buildings with better textbooks and better educated teachers have not made a difference. Since "outcomes" is the operative word in education, what would be the outcome if an adequate assessment were made with current data? Bigger may not be better. It could be the opposite!

EIGHT-GRADE EXAM

Recently a pastor asked a large congregation to stand if they had a college degree. Most of the audience stood. He held a questionnaire and asked them to remain standing if they knew the answer. After reading a few questions no one was standing. The pastor remarked that his questions were taken from an eight grade exam for entrance into the ninth grade in 1911. The college grads could not answer correctly. What does this mean for education today? Was bigger better?

A future book will address the problems of higher education; but suffice it to say the present secondary system is not adequately preparing students for tertiary education. Students arrive as freshmen in college and need a host of remedial courses related to knowledge they should have gained as a prerequisite to a high school diploma.

CHAPTER TWO

Spurious State of Mind

A FALSE MINDSET

In botany, the word "spurious" means like in appearance but unlike in structure or function. The building may look like a church, the sounds coming from inside, music and praise, may be the same as other churches. It has a pastor, or several staff ministers, but is it a real church? It is amazing how churches can appear to be the same, but actually are totally different in organization and programs. The purpose of the church is to equip believers to do the work of ministry and thus edify the Body of Christ. Unless the true purpose of the church is being fulfilled, what happens in a church-type building may only be the function of a social gathering, an exercise in minister-ego, or a selective club for would-be disciples following afar off.

It is surprising how bogus ideas get into culture and the thinking of common folk. Such illegitimate imaginings cannot be traced to a father. Through the years, many spurious concepts have polluted the mindset coming from fables, myths, old wives tales, and simple fabrication. Almost everything has suffered from attempts to counterfeit. The only thing that has been free from the false prophets is the daily moral and ethical life-style of an individual or family. One such case of a false mindset entered my consciousness via El Salvador.

As a minister in South Florida, a missionary asked if my church would take a lady from El Salvador for six months as a domestic. She could work for five church families during the week and for the church on Saturdays. Seeing a pregnant woman cleaning the parsonage, my spirit was troubled and Maria was asked "Why are you here? Why did you leave your husband and four small children and come to America pregnant?" Her humble response shocked me! Maria said in broken English, "In my community the Catholics have a large church building and the people assume their God is bigger than the God of our small church. Because both our church and home are small, I came here to work and save money to buy lumber for my husband to build onto the house and church so people will see our God as being bigger."

This happened in 1962; I was astonished to learn that people could think that the size of the church building or home would be compared to the size of God or the size of God's blessing. The comment was overlooked as the mindset of a small Third World country. However, in the intervening decades, this attitude has taken hold in America. People are building and buying larger and more expensive homes to satisfy their ego and make a statement about affluence. Also, I see the same mindset taking hold in churches. Do people in large churches really reason that God is measured by the size of the church building? Surely not! At last check, God had not changed but is still measured by a personal faith and individual action and not by the dollars in a bank or the square feet in a building.

Dreams and Nightmares

Dreams of growth can turn into a nightmare, because a dream without a workable agenda is just a delusion. One can crave growth in numbers and expend the energy to gain attendance that should be allocated for personal evangelism and care for the souls already in the congregation. There is a barrenness in such a busyness; action without positive results. Growth that is unprecedented can become costly in manpower, material, and money. The worst part of the rapid growth syndrome is that the churches often neglect their real purpose: to equip believers to do the work of the ministry in their family unit and the community where they live and work.

Slow Growth is Natural

Slow growth is natural and permits leadership to grow with the group and perform adequately the service needs of the people; however, a warning sign of some magnitude comes when all the individuals in a group cannot be adequately served by one spiritual leader and there are demands for additional helpers. When one Minister cannot handle the needs for service to a congregation, it is time to consider forming another congregation within the church structure or planting another church for outreach in order to keep the size manageable for one key leader. This would be the natural thing to do. Instead of doing the acceptable thing according to church growth principles, more staff are added and this exacerbates the problem. Why should this be?

Some may not Understand Growth

It is because some clergy do not understand the nature of church growth: new converts and new congregations. The evangelistic activity produces new converts and an understanding of how a church grows permits the development of new congregations within the church. The key here is that these new congregations are to be cared for by deacons and elders and consecrated parents, not paid staff. A major difficulty in this process is handling people who transfer in from other churches or come from other denominations.

Transfer growth can bring into the new church membership individuals who have never trusted Christ as Savior. New people may have new and different doctrines or practices that could cause a root of bitterness (a poison tree) to spring up and cause difficulties for many and serious problems for church leadership. The "things" that caused transfer folk to move to another church, could bring individuals with tainted doctrines, or just serious personal problems that could plant a root of bitterness in the congregation that would grow into a serious problem.

Adding members from other churches is not

true growth; it is called transfer growth, but this is building on the foundation of another. Paul was careful to avoid building on "another man's foundation." (Romans 15:20) Normally, this means that the nature of the conversion and the previous life-style of the new member may not be fully known by the present congregation. At times, this is taking into the church a foreign idea or strange beliefs. It is not that these mobile folk are to be rejected, but that their presence is to be understood. Note this example from a growing church in Atlanta:

One Sunday morning an 80 year old lady came forward to join the church by transfer. It was the same Sunday that my wife and I joined the same church. We were taken back to a conference room and asked several questions about our conversion and spiritual life and basic beliefs. Overhearing the questions put to the elderly lady, she had belonged to eight other Baptist churches, but could not to the Deacons satisfaction explain her conversion or her walk with Christ. What did the Deacon do? He patiently explained that true conversion is a known process and that she must know when and where she asked for and accepted the forgiveness of sins. Her answer continued to be, "I have been a member of the church since I was a little girl and have faithfully attended church through the years." This was not enough. The Deacon continued to work with the woman until she realized she was just a part of the Christian culture, but had never personally claimed Christ for herself. Observing this process, I understood why this particular church was growing,

growing in the right way, and growing stronger. Yes, the woman left that room with a testimony of personal saving grace.

TRUE GROWTH

A church is a social institution and follows the rules of multi-cellular organisms. These natural rules speak to the issue of true growth: all natural growth is by cell enlargement and cell division. Since the church is clearly described as a body, it is abnormal to add a cell that the organism did not produce itself. True church growth translates into new converts and new congregations; not transfer growth by members moving from another church. A mobile society has created a transplanting of members from one church to another and this process has some of the same problems as surgical transplanting of body parts; the foreign body-part is in danger of rejection or creating more liabilities than assets for the body. The spiritual and psychological problems related to transfer growth have not been sufficiently addressed in most case studies.

CLASS VS. CELL

In church growth terms, a congregation is from 40 to 120 persons, gathered on the bases of sameness and fellowship. A congregation may be divided into cells and classes for needs other than fellowship. Cells are circular and intimate and operational with 8 to 12 individuals; when it grows to 16 or more it should be divided or it will not function effectively.

A class may be of any number. Why the unlimited number for a class and limited numbers for a cell?

Because the cell is an intimate and relational unit and a class is a vertical situation meaning the students look vertically to the teacher and the subject of the class rather than horizontally to the people in the class.   A class is a learning environment not a fellowship.   Attempting to make a class into a fellowship unit will destroy the educational value of the class.   This often happens in Sunday school classes when they are turned into fellowship units rather than serious study sessions.

RELATIONSHIP FORMULA (R= N X (N-1) >?

Larger numbers complicate interpersonal relationships; this is what the church is all about.   A believer in fellowship, learning and sharing with others, is the fundamental nature of the church. The formula to determine the number of interpersonal relationships in a group is a simple mathematical equation.   Relationship equals the number times the number minus one or $[R = n \times (n-1) >?]$.   For example, in a group of 40 individuals there are $[40 \times (40-1) > 1{,}560$ interpersonal relationships].   Growth in numbers quickly complicates the fellowship activities of a church.   When the group grows to 120, the formula clearly demonstrates the complexity of the relationship factor. $[120 \times (120 - 1) = 14{,}280$ interpersonal relationships].   It is easy to see how growth can complicate the fellowship function of a church.

COMPLEXITY OF THE RELATIONSHIP FACTOR

When a fellowship group (a congregation) grows beyond 120, it naturally divides into two or more congregations based on age, culture, interest and friendship. This process is automatic whether it is recognized or not. The transfer of individuals from other churches with different backgrounds and cultures complicates the relationship problem. Look at the complex numbers when church attendance reaches 1000. The math would be 1000X 999 = 999,000. If attendance reached 10,000, the math would be: 10,000 X 9,999 = 99,990,000 interpersonal relationships. Of course the Gospel is for everyone and the church must be inclusive; however, New Testament church growth was along homogeneous lines. To grow beyond 120, leaders must understand the complexity of the process and work to maintain an environment conducive to fellowship and worship. This is normally lost in the celebration-type service. Unless leaders understand this, the exit door will be busy.

This does not mean that the church should exclude anyone; it simply means that a growing church must have multiple congregations (fellowship units) and requires additional programming for cells and classes to handle diversity and special interest. A growing church must understand this to keep harmony and a sense of agreement among the people. Of course, everyone can worship together in the Celebration because it is a vertical experience and not dependent on fellowship. Yet, there are liabilities with the celebration-type worship. The leader must understand that the celebration is vertical and not a fellowship service or the value of the function will be lost and the people discomforted or disturbed. Also, the vertical nature of the celebration develops people who are insensitive to the needs of their neighbor.

LOWEST-COMMON-DENOMINATOR RELIGION

One Lord, One Faith, One Baptism has been lost in the pluralism of some growing churches. The New Testament churches were homogeneous fellowships. For example, Jesus was a Galilean, His disciples were Galileans, even Judas was replaced by Mathias, a Galilean, a believer that had been with the group from the beginning. On the Day of Pentecost, the 120 in the Upper Room were perceived to be Galileans. Of course they were not all from Galilee, but they had become acculturated to Jesus of Galilee in their walk and speech. This is not to say that each local church must be made up of one race or culture, but it strongly suggests that all truly converted individuals will develop a common culture and a sameness that breeds close fellowship rather than segregation into various parts of a building complex based only on age, gender, marriage, and other arbitrary pigeon holes. It should be understood that going beyond certain limits of growth creates an entity that is either less than or more than a church. Neither of these options is good for the Christian cause.

CELLS, CONGREGATIONS AND CELEBRATION

When classes, cells, and congregations come together it is called a Celebration and this is a vertical situation with unlimited numbers. The Celebration is unlimited because individuals look vertically to the leader in charge rather than horizontally to their neighbor. This is where the problem begins in the larger gatherings. When individuals are not concerned with others, they become selfish and the personal problems are compounded. Some leaders becomes accustomed to a celebration-mindset, and become oblivious to the needs of individuals. Losing sight of the needs of the congregants diverts the purpose of the church itself. Others who understand the need of the group for fellowship attempt to turn the "celebration" into a congregational fellowship service. This complicates growth by confusing the people as to the function of the major worship service – the vertical Celebration.

The Celebration is a service of worship. Worship is simply attributing worth and value to God and responding vertically to celebrate this value. When congregants in a service of celebration are asked by an uninformed leader to "turn and shake hands with someone" they become distracted from true worship which is vertical. Fellowship is a horizontal function that should be taken care of at the congregation or cell level. Until this is clearly understood a church group will not gather in one place, in one mind, and in one accord to participate vertically in worship and demonstrate the worth and value of God in their lives. Could this be a reason for so many drop-outs from church services?

UNPRECEDENTED, RAPID GROWTH

One can dream and work for growth in an effort to be the biggest and best, but when unprecedented, rapid growth brings challenges; such as, the ability to serve the needs of all the people individually, growth becomes overwhelming. Natural growth should be slow. Fast growth is considered a malignancy and a scourge that causes extra expense of energy and resources and neglect of the basics. Growth follows the multi-cellular organism pattern of enlargement and cell division. If no division exists, only enlargement, then this so called "success" has the seeds of failure and growth becomes a serious problem to long-term viability. In fact the word "success" should never be used with a church function. The operative word is "adequate." Is the church adequate to support one strong spiritual leader and adequate to minister to the needs of each and every individual who submit themselves to the watch-care of a particular church? Success suggests "more than enough" or that someone has "exceeded a goal;" these are not appropriate constructs by which a church or ministry should be assessed.

Remember the story in Luke about servants, "When you have done all those things commanded of you, say, We are unprofitable servants because we have done that which was our duty to do." (Luke 17:10) How can success be assessed in terms of this statement? Doing what is required makes one adequate to the task, but it does not cause one to supersede the task. What about those who attempt to delegate to paid staff by job description the watch-care of souls rightfully assigned by Scripture to the Minister? Surely others can assist in this process; however, one cannot delegate accountability even though responsibility for the task is assigned to another. There is no responsibility without accountability.

~

It is not sufficient to have a good idea; one must understand the consequences of the idea.

CHAPTER THREE

Systematic Syndrome
from Historic Realities

FAILED STRUCTURES AND ADVENTURES

The failed structures and adventures of the past may be instructive for the present and predictive for the future. Those who plan and develop the structures of religious organizations could learn from both Scripture and the historic realities; such as the Titanic disaster, lessons from nature, the normal S-curve of growth, the city-state system, and the American stewpot, America's name brand religion and freeze-frame theology. Also, that the stained-glass and massive buildings pose a psychological barrier that prevents many of the poor from hearing the gospel. This happens when Scripture clearly informs the church that the poor are the easiest people to reach. Why does a Growing Church draw the rich and famous instead of the poor and needy?   Is this a modern-day replica of the old "loaves and fishes" from the time of Jesus or is it just the psychology of following the crowd?

THE CATHEDRAL MINDSET

All the things Protestants complain about Catholicism are being replicated in some super-sized churches today. Construction of massive Cathedrals in Europe created lethargy and boredom and some believe precipitated what is called the "Dark Ages" and eventually required the Reformation. Attendance at services was a guilt trip that denied a man-to-God approach to divine forgiveness. Expected attendance and the obligation to confess to a priest brought a sluggishness and indolence to the people. The vain repetition was a source of monotony and weariness in the spiritual walk and an unholy dependency on human structure for redemption. There was a struggle to remain in good standing or receive the wrath of the church and be denied communion and a burial plot in consecrated ground.

This was organized spiritual abuse, and according to some, it is being replicated in the present super-sized church environment. The new mega-groups pick up the concept of universality with a strong papal-type leadership structure, authoritarian crowd control, ritualistic observance, repetitive programs, and dormant devotees who freely "purchase" the new budgetary indulgence as licenses for a false freedom in behavior. This pattern of behavior conditions congregants to remain passive observers rather than active participants in worship.

NO PREPARATION BY THE PEOPLE

The reasons Martin Luther endured the wrath of German churchmen, with efforts to bring a copy of Scripture to the common man and to proclaim justification by faith, are sufficient grounds to look at the possible implications for a super-sized church with almost total control on the lives of participants. Priests in the Cathedrals were the only ones knowledgeable of scripture text and interpreted the passage to passive spectators. The audience was not equipped with sufficient scriptural knowledge to make the life and death decisions required by the church without direct guidance. Are we growing another crop of church-going folk who cannot think for themselves, but follow blindly those with position and personality?

Aside from the reasons Cathedrals were constructed, the most significant comparison to the present church scene with the Cathedral is the primary Sunday sermon. The church is normally filled with spectators or passive hearers who hear the words but the meaning is not clear; consequently, they continue a life-style not different from those who have no relationship with the church. The speaker is the only person who makes preparation for the message and the words fall on deaf ears. After hours of preparation the minister delivers words that have no knowledgeable hearers and little contact with reality. No one is truly listening and analyzing the message that would generate constructive response and positive action. Why would people not listen to the Word of God? Why have so many who attend church services become God-Evaders?

No Word of Hearing

The scriptural definition of preaching is "the word of hearing." If there were no true listeners; then did anyone hear the message or get the meaning of the words? Perhaps one should ask the old question "If a tree falls in the woods and there is no one to hear the noise, did the tree make a sound?" There must be a receiver in the process of communication. If the sender cannot get the message through the channel because of the static, there is no hearing; therefore, no message. The pews are filled with God-evaders counting the pieces of stained-glass in the windows, the number of panels in the choir blind, the squares in the organ speaker-box, or looking through the Hymnal. As Clyde Reid said five-decades ago, "The American pulpit is empty, no one is listening!" Dr. Reid's statement was made out of doctoral research and before the super-Churches existed in America or the phenomena of American "TV-Evangelists;" surely the facts remain compelling today. What percentage of attendees at the super-Church are God-evaders? Listening requires analysis and action. Do we see such response from the people?

SIZE, WEALTH, AND FAME

Size, wealth, and a crowd of famous people did not make a difference in the Titanic disaster. Many of the plans from the past and the organizations built on the reputation and good name of previous leaders are simply accidents waiting to happen. The laws of nature are ignored. The simple facts of church growth principles are lost in the haste to gain attendance for next Sunday. Relationships built by one generation usually cannot be passed to another. Even religious organizations are made of human design and limited by the human factor. Regardless of the spiritual nature of the enterprise, hard work, and dedicated efforts, historic realities and limitations of the human element are baggage of the past and remain a liability to growing churches that ignore lessons from the past.

PRISTINE HOUSE CHURCHES

The pristine and powerful congregations of the New Testament were small house churches filled with the zeal and power of a first generation experience and led by born again fathers who were the priests of their own households. It is amazing that some churchmen feel they can minister to and care for thousands on the journey toward righteousness when Jesus Himself consistently taught only twelve.   When the crowd grew, Jesus wisely cut it down to size. Certainly here is a lesson worth learning in this fact.

CARE OF SOULS AND ACCOUNTABILITY

The souls of the house-churches were cared for by the Head of the House, as a father caring for his own children. Perhaps the seminaries no longer teach, or the present clergy have forgotten, that they are accountable for the souls under their authority. "Obey them that have the rule over you, and submit yourselves: for they watch for your souls, as they that must give account, that they may do it with joy, and not with grief: for that is unprofitable for you."(Hebrews 13:17)

A PROPER EXEGESIS

When this verse has a proper exegesis, it becomes clear that to "obey and submit" to the authority of a minister who does not demonstrate personal care for your soul is unprofitable.   Not only for the individual members of the congregation, but the community at large suffers when senior leadership evades accountability for primary tasks of the ministry. The care and accountability in this verse is the same as a shepherd who cares for all the sheep. The word for "watch" is an old word meaning to search as a shepherd would sleeplessly seek after a lost sheep. Yet the responsibility for this task is delegated to paid staff while the senior leadership travels around as some super hero. What about the sheep left behind or placed in the care of a novice? Can a "job description" relieve a minister of God called responsibility and accountability?

WATCH-CARE REQUIRED FOR ALL THE PEOPLE

A true church requires watch-care and spiritual supervision. A minister must look diligently, or constantly, to guard the people lest anyone falls behind or becomes a straggler on the journey of faith. This is not a question of basic salvation, but one of participating in living grace and witnessing to the community. Falling behind on the journey can bring the beginning of bitterness. The concept of bitter is used for poison. Concern here is that should some become discouraged or fail to practice their faith and drop out of attendance, it will plant a poisonous tree that could grow and cause many to be in harms way. Should someone hold bad doctrines or become discouraged from participation, it could spread like a prairie fire. Without proper and personal watch-care the poison of negative participation could mean real and expanding trouble for the church. As a result, many may be defiled or contaminated.
(Hebrews 12:12-15)

A GENERAL IS STILL A SOLDIER

A general is still a soldier and must fulfill the basic responsibilities assigned to any member of the Armed Forces. The Shepherd of the flock, in a sense, is also a sheep and must be individually involved with others. Church leaders are also part of the laity and have individual responsibilities as any other believer. Giving oneself to prayer and ministry of the Word without demonstrating a personal concern for those who submit to ministry authority is a serious role conflict. Clergy-leadership must recognize their responsibility and accountability for the welfare of the people. Otherwise, this will ultimately provide evidence of neglect and prove unprofitable for the membership. Such neglect will sow the seeds of malfunction, breakdown, and collapse and is contrary to a "call to ministry."

SPELL MISSIONARY WITH A LITTLE "M"

After the Auca Indian massacre of five young men in Ecuador, correspondence with Elizabeth Elliot taught me some vital lessons. My letter asked several questions about being a Missionary. She responded that one should never capitalize "missionary" because it is the task of all believers, not just the few who journey to a foreign country. From this lesson, it was reasoned that other words related to tasks and roles of spiritual leaders should not be capitalized. Since then, care has been taken to spell the list in Ephesians 4:11 with lower case first letters (apostles, prophets, evangelists, pastors and teachers). There are basic tasks and responsibilities regardless of position or current job description for which a minister is to be held accountable. These cannot be delegated.

EVERYONE IS ACCOUNTABLE

Leadership must always be accountable. In the military and in business there are individuals who refuse a promotion because they did not wish to be responsible for more people. No one feels responsible unless they are accountable to someone. When leadership re-writes their job description to fit a watered-down view of ministry, a congregation is in trouble. In reality, lay people understand this fact.

A story is told of a young pastor of a small church who missed an elderly lady in church. On a visit he asked why she did not attend church. Her answer, "Because of your preaching!" frustrated the minister. He responded, "Is it that bad?" "No it is very good," said the woman. Now the young pastor was really confused and asked, "How could good preaching keep you out of church?" The response, "I already know more Scripture than I want to be accountable for, so I won't be back!" This story clearly illustrates that all are accountable for what they know to do. Although scripture suggested "Where there is no law there is no sin!" In my judgment there is no excuse for a minister not to be involved in the basic tasks where God expects involvement by each and every Believer.

JESUS CUT DOWN HIS CROWD

Jesus actually attempted to cut down the size of His crowd. When one notes the facts related to the ministry of Jesus, they see a concern for quality not quantity. Jesus saw the crowd as following for the "loaves and fish." On one occasion, only three disciples remained and Jesus told them to go away, too. Peter declared "Where are we going to go, you have the Words of Life;" consequently, the decision of Peter, James, and John to stay near to Christ was honored. This was an effort to improve the quality and exactly the opposite of growth in numbers. When considering the quality of Christian commitment in the context of some growing churches, it is no wonder so many leaders fail to achieve their lofty goals. Why then the large crowds in some churches? Are people seeking to be lost in the crowd? Are they just spectators attending for the loaves and fishes?

QUALITY BUILDING MATERIAL

When a Growing Church stands alone without account- ability to others and follows the practice of self- comparison, it neglects the words Saint Paul wrote to the Corinthians: "measuring themselves by themselves and comparing themselves among themselves, are not wise." Without the extended brotherhood for balance and correction, any and all local congregations are in jeopardy. (2 Corinthians 10:12b)

IT IS GOD'S SALT

A Growing Church must not forget that "Numbers" is a Book in the Old Testament and that numbering Israel was considered a great sin because it showed a lack of trust in God's deliverance. The Book of Acts (of the Apostles) is the New Testament example. Not piling up God's salt all on one corner when it is clear from Scripture that the salt of saints should be distributed throughout the community for the cure of souls. Has the leadership forgotten their primary duty is to care for souls and to give an account for this action?

LIGHT OF THE WORLD

Also there is the problem of light. Since Believers are the light of the world, why would some want to bottle up the light into one laser-type beam? Light is life giving and the spiritual glow of the saint is the candle of the Lord to guide one to walk in agreement with the Scripture. Should this light become concentrated into one laser-type beam; it can become destructive. This is especially true when this light is in the hands of weak leaders and/or a group that cannot adequately defend itself against criticism.

DANGEROUSLY POWERFUL

Although laser light is visible in daylight, the infrared beam is brief, dangerously powerful and truly destructive in the wrong hands. The laser gives light a longer range, but the dangers are compounded. God gives each believer a connection to the light-source and the command is clear: "Let your light so shine before men that they may see your good works and glorify your heavenly Father."(Matthew 5:16) God never intended the collective light of believers to be used to advance a local ministry or impress a television audience.

VICTORY AT GILBOA

Gilboa was a significant place in Israel's military history; it is the site of Saul's great defeat resulting from his dis- obedience and Gideon's great victory based on simple obedience. It was at Gilboa where the Lord instructed Gideon to reduce his forces from 32,000 to 300 men so that it would be obvious that God was responsible for the upcoming victory.

Gideon, a great warrior, was willing to lead the great mass of volunteers into battle, but God wanted the credit for the future victory. To assure this, Gideon was told, "the people that are with you are too many." Gideon obeyed and cut down the size of his army and the Lord and Gideon's tiny band of 300 routed the enemy and God received the credit. It is clear from Scripture that 300 watchful warriors can achieve a spiritual victory that could elude 32,000 fearful and careless volunteers. (Judges 7:1-25) Does this speak to a Growing Church?

Obedience Brought Victory

Gideon's obedience brought victory in one of the most remarkable conflicts of Israel's history. The people had been cruelly oppressed as the result of disobedience. It was clear that their deliverance should be evident by divine action. It would have been disastrous for them to imagine they were able to extricate themselves from the circumstances in the midst of suffering and weakness without divine intervention.

By divine direction, Gideon was ordered to sift the army. Thirty-two thousand willing souls had responded to the call to fight; however, the results of Gideon's tests showed they lacked the positive attitude necessary to achieve victory in the forthcoming battle. The first test was to allow all who were faint-hearted or afraid to return home. Twenty-two thousand turned away from the battle fearful of the fight, but 10,000 were still too many for God to get the credit for the upcoming victory.

The number was too large, because in God's eyes
quality is more important than quantity. A simple test
for the remaining 10,000 revealed that the many were
not sufficiently aware of the imminent danger to be
trustworthy. An ambush might surprise them. The
men who stooped and drank water from their hand
were watchers as well as fighters. Such men took no
unnecessary time over necessary things and proved to
be the men who were needed. Nine thousand seven
hundred more returned home leaving a handful of
three hundred brave souls. Now God can give the
victory.

Have we forgotten that God does not count
attendance or look at budgets, but discerns the
attitude of the heart and chooses those wise and
watchful worshipers to be Christian soldiers in the
battle against evil? It appears that 300 is the magic
number that God will bless. Is this 300 men, not
counting women and children? Perhaps! Then
that would push the number up to about 900 to
1,000. Honestly, that number is pushing the growth
envelope for being accountable for the individuals
involved.

~

CHAPTER FOUR

Skeptical Signs from the Titanic

THE TITANIC SYNDROME

The whole world knows about the sinking of the Titanic and recently the public has learned more about the possible cause of the worst disaster in maritime history. Why call this disaster a "syndrome?" A syndrome is from the Greek "a running together." When a number of symptoms run or occur together they characterize a specific disease in the medical sense; thus, a syndrome.

From a more technical view, a syndrome is a set of signs that together indicate the presence of an abnormal condition. Each set of signs is considered a symptom or a warning indicator of future malady, disorder, dysfunction, or difficulty. A syndrome has atypical, nonstandard, and uncharacteristic signs which decoded become a secret language for analysis and diagnosis. There certainly is a secret coded message coming from the bottom of the sea from a rusting, decaying Titanic, the unsinkable ship.

STIPULATED FACTS CREATE A SYNDROME

It is the assumption that the stipulated facts create a syndrome and if adequately analyzed could produce beneficial applications for other mega-ventures. The term "mega" has been applied to many things: a large city, a large sum of money, big businesses, and to large areas of the world. The term could easily describe the super-sized churches of the 21st Century. The Titanic owners, the architects, the builders, the financiers, the passengers all behaved (ti-tan'i-cal-ly) in an adverbial manner. Could this be applied to the behavior of people involved with large churches today? Are they blindly steering through troubled waters with a near capacity load without caution or benefiting from the Titanic lessons? Are the signal operators on neighboring ships fast asleep? Has the Captain and crew ignored warnings of trouble ahead?

THE MEANING OF "TITANIC"

Understanding the meaning of the word "titanic" chosen for the Olympic class mega-ship is the first clue of trouble. The dictionary definition of "ti-tan-ic" is revealing: having great stature or enormous strength; huge or colossal; of enormous in scope, power, or influence; of great force or power. The definition continues—big, large, above average in size or number or quantity or magnitude or extent. The RMS Titanic was called a Mega-Ship because the definition adequately describes the reason "titanic" was chosen as the name. The meaning of "mega" is also descriptive of the "extra-large, jumbo, mammoth, super" ship and the giant-sized egos of the people involved.

THE MEGA-SHIP WAS NONSTANDARD

The sinking of the RMS Titanic provided signs in the cryptic language of propositions that the ship was nonstandard, and characteristically atypical. Warning indicators of future difficulties were obviously built into the ship itself. Regardless of what the scientist and naval architects, sonar experts, microbiologist or historians of the shipwreck finally determine the primary cause of the disaster, from the existing data the world knows the flawed unsinkable, ship was certainly sinkable. In fact a sea-worthy lifeboat was safer in the icy waters of the North Atlantic than the Titanic on Sunday 14 April 1912.

AN ARROGANT ATTITUDE RELATED TO THE BIG SHIP

The name chosen for the ship, "Titanic" was the first indicator of the arrogant attitude of the primary people and the future problems related to size. The RMS Titanic was 882 feet 9 inches long and 92 feet 6 inches at the beam. The Gross Tonnage was 46,328 tons and a height from the water line to the boat deck of 60 feet. The Titanic was arrogant in design. Of the four large 63 foot funnels, only three were functional, the fourth was added to make the ship look more impressive. Those who observed the actual sinking probably did not think it so impressive. The price some paid to be a part of the Titanic disaster was certainly not a bargain and the trip was not worth the price. The old saying, "Price is forgotten when quality is remembered." The survivors and the families of those lost most certainly remembered the price and forgot the quality.

MEASURED BY OLD STANDARDS

At the time of the sinking, RMS Titanic was the largest passenger steamship in the world. This was a short lived achievement! The Titanic could carry 3,547 passengers and crew, and since the ship carried the mail, it was given the title Royal Mail Steamer: thus, RMS Titanic. The super-Ship was considered the pinnacle of naval architecture and technological achievement and thought to be unsinkable. It was larger and more sophisticated, but was it safe? The old standards and codes by which the Titanic was built were far behind the times and the materials were not up to the vision of the builders.

LIFEBOAT SAFER THAN THE MEGA-SHIP

Although the Titanic exceeded the current standard of 20 lifeboats, the ship sailed with lifeboats for only half the passengers and 68 percent of the passengers and crew were lost. Following legal rules of the day was not sufficient. The Titanic struck an iceberg 20 minutes before midnight on Sunday 14 April 1912 and sank in just 2 hours and 40 minutes early Monday morning on 15 April. What if the Mega-Ship had been successful in filling all 3,547 passenger slots? With the lifeboat situation many more would have been lost. It is obvious that a sea worthy lifeboat was safer than the unsinkable ship. It is also clear that a larger number on the passenger list would have appeared more successful, but the disaster would have been worse. Can we learn anything from this? Larger and seated to capacity super-churches may not be better than the small community church that served as a life-boat church for many families through the years.

A SPIRIT OF COMPETITION

There was evident competition to be the largest and most luxurious ship ever to operate and to compete with a rival company's line of luxurious ships, who at the time were the fastest liners on the Atlantic. The prideful expectation was to be the biggest and fastest and most luxurious on the high seas. The building of the Titanic was supported by the rich and famous, successful in their professional life, but somewhat limited in the science of ship building especially for passenger service. For the rich and famous to be associated with the Titanic project, either as supporters or passengers, speaks directly to a competitive spirit. Why do the rich and famous flock to the new super-churches and forget their simple roots? Why do the poor feel unwelcome or out of place in such places? Remember, the poor hear the Gospel gladly and when the poor and needy fail to attend that is a warning sign of trouble ahead.

THE UNSINKABLE SHIP

The ship had been declared unsinkable because of 16 watertight compartments divided by open doors held up in the open position by electro-magnetic latches that could be closed by a switch on the ship's bridge and a back-up system where the doors could be closed by a float system in case of rising water. Neither system was used because the nature of the damage was unforeseen. It was not the vastness of the damage, but the location. It seems that the quality of the steel of that day had too much sulfur and was breakable in cold water. It is also clear that the ship building material did not match the architect's vision.

OBVIOUS COMMON SENSE OVERLOOKED

The Titanic was on a maiden voyage and with an untried crew for such a large ship. In fact, the crew was experienced on smaller ships, but most had no experience on a super-ship. The Captain ignored radio transmission warning of icebergs and investigators found the ship was steaming too fast in dangerous waters. Another ship was close by, the California, but the radio operator was off duty and asleep. The Titanic sailed under a ruse, it flew a British flag and had British registry, but was owned by a US company controlled by the financier J. P. Morgan. Sounds a little like some of the super-churches operate under a d.b.a. or an innovative name that hides the identity of a sectarian connection or doctrinal position; thus, they fail to declare the basic teachings they espouse. Claiming this is a marketing tool, but in reality it is false advertising. Is this any different than the Titanic advertising that it was the biggest and best and surely unsinkable?

FEW HASTY CHANGES

The disaster precipitated a few hasty changes in Maritime Law, but the changes represented obvious safety concerns that were well known by anyone who went to the sea in ships. The few reforms included: (1) lifeboat space for everyone on board was instituted; (2) regular lifeboat drills were to be organized; (3) a full-time radio watch must be maintained at sea, and (4) an international Ice Patrol was established. This was too little, too late to be of assistance to the HMS Titanic passengers and crew.

Planners Made Small Changes

The planners were to build three big ships and searched for names to represent the ship builder's dreams. Three names were chosen for the fleet of three Mega-Ships in the Star Line: Olympic, Titanic, and Gigantic. Of the three super-Ships, the Olympic was the only vessel of the trio of Olympic-class ship that actually managed to perform her assigned duty to carry passengers. Only one of the big ships succeeded. That means two-thirds failed in their mission because of their enormous size and the built-in flaws in the structural design.

Few Lessons Learned

After the Titanic sank it somewhat sobered the builders and the name Gigantic was changed to Britannic. Changing the name of the next ship – a disaster by any other name is the same gigantic mess. The Britannic became a Royal Hospital Ship and never became a regular passenger ship. Although the Titanic stayed afloat nearly 3 hours, the Britannic sank within 45 minutes after a German U-Boat torpedo did fatal damage. The sinking of the Britannic demonstrated that few lessons had been learned from the Titanic disaster. In roughly 45 minutes after a single deadly explosion the largest British-built ship afloat had vanished, leaving behind 35 lifeboats and a scattering of derby on an empty sea. If they learned a lesson from the sinking of the Titanic, they did not heed the warning signs for the next mega-disaster.

Most of the watertight doors did not work, the port holes were left open contrary to regulations, and the Captain turned the ship after the explosion and tried to speed to shallow water but only increased the taking on of water through the open portholes. Also, although there were sufficient lifeboats, they were deployed badly and most of the 30 causalities were in the first two lifeboats launched prematurely and sucked under the propeller of the sinking ship. It appears difficult to learn lessons from a disaster. Everyone is caught up in the emotion that the meaning and value of the facts evade reality. Could many growing churches be ignoring data that could bring on a disaster?

ANALYSIS WITHOUT APPLICATION

Several decades passed before the actual wreck of the Titanic was found (1973) at a depth of 12,000 feet. In 1998 a section of the ship's outer hull was recovered for investigation and the world continues to learn about the possible causes of the disaster. Movies, books, websites, and memorials all share facts applied retrospectively about the people and the builders. Has the world learned enough from the known facts to extrapolate to other cases? Is it possible on the basis of existent data to identify the antecedent signs and describe a syndrome that may exist in other human endeavors? Have experts only analyzed the data and not made specific application to other aspects of human attempts to be the biggest and the best in spite of the obvious dangers.

CHAPTER FIVE

Sober Clues from the Multicultural Stew Pot

LESSONS FROM THE MULTICULTURAL STEW POT

The often acclaimed American melting pot does not exist. Generations have been poured into this pot and have not lost their identity; they refused to melt. Maintaining their ethnic identity and marks of National origin they remain visible in the population. All the effort to bring people together in a pluralistic society ultimately becomes a mixture of culture, language, and race, a virtual human stew pot. In a stew pot all the elements are identifiable: a potato remains a potato, celery is still recognized, onions are visible, and the meat remains. Together they flavor each other, but retain their identity.

A NONCHALANT LIFESTYLE

Many church going individuals unintentionally hinder the conversion of the next generation by a nonchalant lifestyle and an indifferent attitude about religion and spiritual things. This is the continuing effect of the multicultural stew pot that produces certain constraints of political correctness, and breeds resistance to the dominant culture. Yet, this multicultural stew pot boils over into the church and restricts fellowship and unity. The larger the pluralistic mix becomes within the church and the more individuals are required to accept differences to be politically correct, the more it complicates communication and communion. While the message may be unity, the emphasis is on significant difference. Quantity and quality are mutually exclusive. Increasing one decreases the other.

THE SIMMERING MESS

The church calls for conversion, a total change of mind, heart, and lifestyle, but most things stay the same. There is little difference in the multicultural stew pot in American society and the simmering mess that spills over into the church. The church is filled with mixed messages, exploited motives, deceitful manners, manipulated memories, and dysfunctional members as much as the cesspool of society. This leads to fraudulent marriages and a restricted spiritual outreach. Christian fellowship becomes a contradiction of terms. The same attitudes that people have in the community about race, culture, food, music and clothing are carried over into the church. This causes disagreement and challenges the core values of Christianity.

Morally and ethically the public sees little difference in church members when they are compared to the general public. This lack of significant difference actually hinders the united voice of the church and weakens any effort to reach the younger generation. The larger the crowd the more difficult it becomes to police individual morality. It is easy to follow the multitude to do evil.

America was once thought to be the great melting pot of the world where all races, creeds, and cultures could become blended into a pristine commonality. This was called the American dream. It was a dream not a goal; no one could develop an agenda to reach this dream.

NO WORKABLE PLANS

The difference between a dream and a goal is an agenda. No workable plans existed to produce the melting pot. It is illusive and unattainable. One wonders if it were ever a realistic goal, because no actual agenda was ever articulated. There was only the vague hint that everything in American would be better. This required work, but the dream fizzled into a welfare state where no one is willing to do an honest days work for wages when they can sit at home and draw a welfare check. The Statue of Liberty invited the teaming masses of the world to the shores of America. They came, but they brought their race, creed, culture, and their own dreams. The big dream took a back seat to private aspirations. Everyone was so busy building his or her own private fantasy; the corporate dream became a nightmare and perished in a slow and agonizing death.

Private aspirations mostly related to individual success or providing better for the next generation. Diplomats and politicians spoke of life, liberty, and the pursuit of happiness, but no agenda was provided to bring everyone aboard the American Ark of Liberty. Many were left behind. Some left behind were the guests of Miss Liberty herself. Others were the sick and suffering, homeless and hungry, also the men and women who suffered the wounds of wars were forgotten in the struggle to reach the impossible dream. Those excluded from the marketplace of work or ideas, looked to the church for hope and inclusion, but the church was too busy building buildings, raising budgets, paying staff salaries to be actively involved in assisting the community.

THE SUBLIMINAL MESSAGE

The true intent of inclusion is lost in the subliminal message of the architecture, the program, and the general atmosphere of the local congregation. Churches also produce a stew pot rather than a melting pot. The ethnic and culturally based denominational structure of Protestantism is sectarian and contributes to the multicultural stew pot. The church fails to demonstrate the central idea that the good news of the gospel is for everyone. The little kingdoms established to protect a particular cultural expression of religion sends the wrong message to the masses. A failure to agree on doctrine and polity contributes to the mixed message and suggests exclusivity for most congregations. The unintended message is one of exclusion. The Christian church should be inclusive. Surely the church would receive everyone in the House of God, but many feel unwelcome.

Tragically, in the minds of many, the church gradually became a sanctuary for the charlatan. The House of Prayer became the place to sit and be preached to or preached at, until everyone turned a deaf ear to the message and the messenger. It was as if the people were wandering in a wilderness of mixed messages, false advertising, crooked politicians, broken promises, shattered families, and depleted dreams. Reality has redefined the American dream and the people are awash in the stew pot and a multi-cultural cesspool. Although there is token allegiance to equality, in reality each group sees their culture and practices as superior and all others inferior to their own.   Even where a common Christian culture develops it is tainted with sectarianism until Christian unity is fractured into exclusive structures.

A STEAMING SOCIAL STEW POT

America did not become the great melting pot; the United States of America became either a stagnant cesspool or a steaming social stew pot, depending on one's point of view. Some would argue the degradation of the vision needs both the figure of a cesspool and the metaphor of a stew pot adequately to define the current moral and social situation.

A stew pot is a covered pot placed over simmering heat and gradually brought to a low boiling point. Many mothers to prepare nourishing meals for the family used such a stew pot. Many have survived the hard times though the use of the old stew pot. Despite the stew pot's value in feeding the family, it is the most defining designation for the American Ark of Liberty, because this ark is filled with many distinct kinds of people all mixed and simmering together. Although the people are blended together as a whole, there are clusters of identifiable groups and these groups have maintained identify over time. Pride of culture and the continuation of valued traditions push the construct of difference and division.

Each item in a stew pot maintains its identity. Potatoes are still potatoes; the carrots, the onions, the celery, and the stew meat itself are all distinguishable. Yet each adds flavor and seasoning to the others. Together they become something more than they were divided. America is similar in many ways to the stew served on the dinner table. This social stew pot is simmering. The churches of bible days and the churches of history had differences based on cultural and ethnic understandings, but there was sufficient common ground in Christ to bring a sense of fraternity. Each group was permitted to worship God in the framework of their own culture. The church in Jerusalem was different from the church in Antioch. The believers in Corinth were not the same kind of folk as the believers in Ephesus. The countries of Europe managed to maintain a national heritage and these national differences are seen in the churches of America.

IN DIVERSITY THERE IS UNDERSTANDING

God always reached individuals within the context of their culture and did not force social change but in certain aspects of acceptable moral practices. It is clear in scripture that a first century gentile did not have to become a Jew to embrace the Christian way. Likewise, a Hebrew did not have to give up the Jewish heritage to accept Jesus as the Messiah. In diversity there is understanding and in commonalties there is strength.

Individuals in a marriage contract remain culturally attached to the family of origin while establishing a new entity and family identity. Likewise, various cultural and ethnic groups within America maintained differences at some levels, but unity at the ultimate measure of devotion to democracy. In many respects the nation has been more effective in this area than the churches. Why must minor differences in doctrine and polity that are culturally based keep different Protestant churches from embracing the common ground in Christianity? The birth pangs of Protestantism was simply "the just shall live by faith." Why now must different books of discipline and polity divide the church?

President Jimmy Carter had some difficulty with the press and others when he attempted to explain the diversity of the multicultural population. Carter expressed a belief that life was not always fair, and argued for the right of different cultural and racial groups to maintain their ethnicity. Scholars agree with President Carter that the music, art, language, food, clothing, and other aspects of ethnic culture and religious expression are important to each group. Ancestry, history, and social background are all a part of one's heritage. Americans are proud of both their heritage and their differences. These make the United States of America a strong and viable democracy. Why do religious leaders, who are enjoined to even "love their enemies" and to "pray for those who despitefully use them" not find strength in diversity? Why can they not agree to disagree agreeably and move forward with a common message? The answer is clear: to move together there must be unity of mind and spirit: one accord in one place.

THE EXISTANCE OF A CULTURAL LAG

Scholars also admit the existence of a cultural lag when one part of a population fails to keep pace with the changes in other related aspects, such as the advances in technology and science. Cultural lag and limited education could explain some simmering in the stew pot. Ethnicity and culture are better explanations for the difference in groups than race or religion. Not only do these areas explain some differences within the population of the country, research has confirmed that ethnic, cultural, or national origins are also the underpinning elements in denominational differences in America. In reality, the church has become a product of the pluralistic society in America.

Just as the foundation stones of democracy and capitalism have been both an asset and a liability to the American dream, the church has been plagued by the diversity that comes from ethnicity or national origin. In a pluralistic society the dichotomy is often the rich and the poor, the employer and the employee, the landlord and the lodger. The dichotomy suggests that American is a house divided and that is an unstable condition. The church is no less divided: one Lord, one Faith, one Baptism--but 300 Protestant denominations. Within these denominations, it has been suggested that more than 21,000 different interpretations of basic Christian doctrine exist. It appears that both America as a Nation and Protestant Christianity as a whole, are simmering stew pots.

Protestant churches emerged in America as a by product of ethnicity and social pluralism. No acceptable national Christian identity has ever existed; consequently, the nation was built more by the forces of democracy, capitalism, and global crisis, than upon any underpinning based on the faith of the founding fathers. The Christian trumpet is sounding so many different calls from so many corners that the people do not know where to assemble. Will anyone follow an uncertain trumpet to battle? When the National resolve was limited and the mission was unclear, many refused to follow the government and the military into Vietnam or Iraq.

A KIND OF SANCTIFIED PATRIOTISM

Even rats desert a sinking ship.   Why has the church been unable to reach successive generations? Perhaps it is because of cognitive dissent among the constituency of Christianity. Many do not believe what their church teaches. Faith inside the church is not much more than a kind of sanctified patriotism. In some areas basic faith about life and living is higher among those who do not attend church. In fact, some clergy who are required to sign theological statements regularly do so with mental reservation. Cognitive dissents although passive in nature is militantly aggressive in its effect on the advance of the church and society.

Management theory presents the dangers of leaders failing fully to agree with corporate or group goals. Even the slightest hint that the leader does not embrace a particular position will be recognized and will have an ill effect. In fact, this kind of dissent is discernible by the senses; it cannot be hidden. Many people have a kind of intuition when a little voice inside speaks up and warns them of inconsistencies in the lives of spiritual leaders. The church itself is a kind of stew pot of beliefs and practices that are not always understood by the public.

Mixed Motives and Mixed Messages

There are mixed motives among those who attend church and mixed messages coming from the pulpits. The multiplicity of messages with the miscellaneous meanings has so confused the teachings of the church until accepting the faith of the fathers is difficult for the young. In fact, even the rationale for the word "believe" has changed; instead of expressing faith at times it expresses doubt or uncertainty. For example, when one is not sure of the weather the uncertain prediction could be "I believe it might rain." When one gives direction, but is doubtful about the details, the explanation could be, "Go three lights, no I believe it is four. Then turn left for two blocks, no I believe it is three . . . Who could follow such directions? This is exactly what the public is hearing from the various churches. "Come here; go there. Go this way; go that way. Do this; do that. Just believe. Give up...turn loose...hold on. Pray and believe. Wait on the Lord. Confess. Be baptized. Join the church. Believe. These are unrealistic expectations not related to biblical reality.

The early approach to evangelism was friendship. Individuals would bring their family and friends to Christ. It is no wonder the scripture explained that one does not come to Christ without the assistance of the Holy Spirit. One needs divine assistance to make any sense out of the mixed message given by American Christianity. Christians are caught up in the notion that their denomination has built a better loading ramp for the Old Gospel Ship than anyone else. Consequently, they preach an exclusive message and reach only a few.

A THEOLOGY OF COERCION

Some "believe" their particular plan will work wonders and cause secular society to beat a path to their church door. Others think a specific interpretation of a theological construct is so precise and correct that if it were taught everyone would believe. Some have a kind of theology of coercion that permits almost any effort or procedure to get someone to agree to a specific approach is acceptable. A recent New England congregation in their zeal to reach the inner city was taken to court because a neighborhood claimed, "They were bribing the kids with pizza." Whatever works....put a few pizzas in the stew pot.

Both the blended church and the blended family have become a multicultural stew pot. Parents are one reason the present generation has turned off the mixed message of the church. The hypocritical lifestyle, the blatant immorality, the obvious unhappiness, all expresses the failure of the family unit. Since families are the building blocks of the church, the family is a reflection of the church itself. When controversy and friction are present in the home, it complicates the witness of Christianity.

When only one parent is interested in the Christian way of life, the children are further confused. Children often think, if being a Christian were so great surely dad would be interested. In fact, believers having children by unbelieving spouses have produced a kind of contaminated generation. This infection has grown into a social epidemic of drugs, gangs, and savage violence. The intensity of family dysfunction has changed both society and the church. The stew pot is simmering.

Hope for the Future Generations

St. Paul wrote to an immoral church in a depraved society and identified part of the problem. The Corinthian church, the most immoral of the congregations described in the New Testament, was given Paul's personal evaluation about the problem of believers living with unbelievers. It was apparent to Paul that Christian converts must sanctify or "separate" their unbelieving spouse from the immorality of the Corinthian society or their children would be under a serious strain. Paul used the Greek grammatical construction (perfect indicative passive) form for the word "separate." Paul clearly asserted a fact that the action of separation from the immorality of Corinthian society had been a process and was completed; consequently, the next generation would be saints. This was an expression of hope for the future generations.

The implied injunction was that Christians ought not to be forced to live with unbelievers unless the spouse was willing to separate from the immorality of society. Otherwise it would bring anxiety and

controversy within the home because the unbelieving mate did not share the consecration of the spouse. Without this reformation in the life of the unbelieving spouse, living together, as husband and wife would produce children that would be difficult to convert to Christianity. Could this be one explanation for the evils of the present generation and the difficulty the church has of reaching them with the gospel?
Paul was predictive of the quality of the children of two parents following the same consecration. His assertion was that they would be blameless and consecrated worthily to be called saints. Even in the mist of an immoral society, Paul believed the next generation could be reached with the gospel. Is this not an indictment against the despair rampant in the church? Since the church has given up on the next generation, where does the church begin to carry out the Great Commission to make disciples?

Worship has Degenerated to entertainment

The uncertain call of the gospel trumpet does not rally the troops within the church or cause much concern outside the walls. Worship has degenerated to entertainment to attract attendance, but the church cannot compete with television, movies, or the Internet surfers. Christian terminology has not been defined by action. Also, the social stew pot has allowed cultural interpretations to divide the various groups of Christians based on the cultural interpretations of church teachings. Another factor is that the theological constructs of the church have been placed in the ambiguity of the English language that has an either/or complex and leaves little room for middle ground in matters of faith and practice. This leads to a lack of inclusiveness; in fact, it bred exclusivity and eliminated many from the influence of the Christian lifestyle.

Just as the biblical Israelites, the church has become sidetracked in the pluralistic wilderness on the way to the American dream. The Israelites wandered for forty years until all of the disobedient generation died, only then was the next generation permitted to cross into the Promised Land. Journeying out of Egypt the Israelites witnessed the miracles of God. Based on the promises of God regarding deliverance, the bones of Joseph were taken from Egypt to the family burial site across the Jordan, but the people were denied entrance to the land that flowed with milk and honey. This denial came because of fear and timidity: fear of the walled cities and the giants in the land and timid in claiming the promises of God to give them the land.

Twelve spies were sent to evaluate the possibilities. Ten came back with a report of gloom and despair. Two claimed that Israel and the God of Israel were well able to possess the land. The majority refused to take the enabling step of faith and behave, as the Children of God should act: take the first step by faith in the direction of the promise and claim victory. Joseph had done just that many years before. At his death Joseph reminded the Israelites that God would visit them and deliver them safely to the Promised Land. Joseph's bones made it. Joshua and Caleb, the two spies with the minority report, made it. Those who would not act, wandered as the People of God, but perished in the wilderness without claiming their promised possession. This sounds a little like the American church.

The Protestant church is marked by frustration, mediocrity, failure, and wandering in the wilderness of a secular society. Public sins, private defeat, abject loneliness, broken relationships and paralyzing depression characterize many church members. Yet there are a few such as Joshua and Caleb who gives the minority reports. God uses the child. God uses the small and insignificant things to effect His purpose provided those God chooses to use are willing to take the risk and make the steps of faith.

Society Pushed the Equality Button

The multicultural stew pot of American has pushed the equality of individuals.   Minorities and women have been given certain advantages in an effort to overcome generations of white male domination. Just a few years back it could be said, "It is a man's world." Although Christianity liberated women and made a claim that "In Christ there was neither male nor female, bond or free." The New Testament era was one of slavery and male dominance.   In fact, the church took the cue from the society of the day, and created a male leadership. Only a few women were able in the early days to secure opportunities for ministry and leadership within the church. However, as society began to push the equality button, the church reluctantly accepted women.

The willingness of the church to accept more female leadership grew more out of a lack of men than an effort to advance women. Notwithstanding the actual reasons for opening the door to women, there has developed a kind of feminization of the church. This sends the wrong signal to men, who are already in short supplied. The message, although unintentional, communicates that the church can get along without men. This is no more the case than it is in the family.

SEND THE RIGHT MESSAGE TO MEN

Some families survive without a father, but the message to the children is confused as to the role of the father. This complicates ones view of God the Father. Research demonstrates that one normally attributes the same qualities to God the Father as are attributed to ones biological father. Growing up without a father has complicated evangelism in the inner city. On one effort the literature had to be changed to place an emphasis on Jesus as the Big Brother rather than God as Father. The church must be careful in the effort to give women a rightful role in advancing the church; care must be taken to send the right message to the men.

Failure of the church to take some of the responsibility for the failure in families also complicates the problem. The bitterness and alienation with the dysfunctional family is normally transferred to the church. Often people in the church take sides when a marriage is dissolved. This multiplies the problems of the two families already caught in the confusion of broken contracts, failed relationships, wounded children, and divided observers who watch, take sides, and shout advice as if they were at some sporting event. This creates wounded and scarred individuals who do not feel they can turn to the church for comfort or sanctuary.

The church purports to be a place filled with mercy and understanding, but the steaming stew pot clouds the manifestation of these virtues; consequently, the image of the House of God is tarnished. Often the most grievous wounds are received in the house of friends. It has been said that the church is the only army that shoots its wounded. Certainly the action of many creates a pessimistic atmosphere in which forgiveness is difficult.

ANIMOSITY AND BITTERNESS

This lack of forgiveness contaminates the very soul of the congregation. Many wounds received in relationship battles leave psychological scars that affect the self-concept of the wounded. This often causes both individuals and groups affected by the war of words to hold animosity and bitterness for years. When this occurs, everyone including the ministry of the church endures great affliction. It becomes clear that the family, the community and the church are interrelated and what happens in one affects the others. Each is affected by the larger society and each other. As the family goes, so goes the church. When the community deteriorates, the church usually follows. When the church is strong, families are strengthened, and communities become better places in which to live and bring up children.

Yet, in the midst of the confusion there are a
few individuals, families and churches that have
prevailed. They are growing, reaching out, sending
missionaries, and growing a new generation of
Christians. These few churches seem to have the old
American "can do" attitude, the vast opportunities
are seen and the courage and faith to work together
in the Name of Christ is working. Just how many
and how long this will work cannot be predicted,
but these have crossed the social Jordan of despair,
breached the immoral walls of the secular cities, and
embrace the inhabitants as redeemed friends. These
few have claimed their community as their parish and
are ministering grace to all that will receive.

The organized church has problems as a whole,
but individually there is hope! There is hope because
Christians who worship and fellowship together
develop a common Christian culture. As each one
accepts another; they all become part of the common
Christian culture. This is complicated by large
numbers. Remember the formula for relationship is
R=n(xn-1). (See Chapter Two) This is why bigger is
not better!

BEST BASE OF OPERATION

Any defense of the viability of Christianity based
on the future of a Growing Church is to say the
structures of the past provide no lessons for today
and the future.   This is certainly not true in any
other aspect of life or history. The church is people
and the basic needs of people do not change. The
church exists in a society, and societies change. This
excuse is used to justify a Growing Church, but

Christ does not change nor does the simple message of salvation. The communication of the Gospel must remain simple and clear in the marketplace. It must not be bottled up in some cathedral-type building that speaks of man's achievement rather that God's grace. According to Scripture, the way of holiness is so plain that a "wayfaring fool would not err there in!" A small family-type, community-based church remains the best base of operation to reach a community and advance Christianity.

Unbelievers not won by Mass Media

Christianity must not depend on the Mega-Church to propagate the Gospel. The structure, message and communication of Christianity must be shared by individual believers as they go about their daily lives. In times past the radio did a sufficient job of reaching people. Radio and television are drastically different mediums. Radio is considered an active (hot) medium where individuals must participate.   The listener uses imagination and can "see" with the mind's eye what they hear; they hear "Hi Oh, Silver!" and subconsciously perceived a horse and masked rider. The listener hears the horse running and clearly received the image.

Television is different.

Television on the other hand is a passive (cool) medium and there is no interactivity, no response — except the ads or the "send me a letter offer" to raise funds. It should be noted that the Christian message was never clearly propagated to the multitudes by mass media: it worked best one on one.   Israel was clearly told, "Thou shalt not follow a multitude to do evil." The world will never be won by mass media or by a few Mega-Churches; there must be the personal involvement of individuals in a daily witness flowing out of a life-style that speaks of the love and grace of divine forgiveness.

THE LAW OF MORTIGRESSION

According to William G. Justice there is a Law of Mortigression that is self-evident. It speaks clearly that all living things move toward death. In Living Systems Theory, James Greer Miller called this construct "time" or "the clock." This is a natural law that is applicable to all living organisms and social institutions. There is consistent movement toward decline, disease and death. Does it apply to the church? It applies to both the church as an organization and to the individuals who make up the church; however, the progressive decline of Christianity is not inevitable. Christianity may be renewed with new converts that bring first generation zeal to the cause. As believers grow in grace and knowledge and participate in a meaningful life-style Christianity is strengthened.

CHANGING THE BUILDING CHANGES THE MESSAGE

Many individual Christians are living their faith effectively and some local congregations are alive and reaching their communities. This is not true in every community, but moving to a building located in another community may not change things. Churches seem to be fragmented, stagnant, and unable to communicate a unified message to the public. Why is this? Probably they get their data from some sectarian source and it is not adapted to the local community. This failure to meet the needs of individuals breeds discontent and negative participation. Ultimately this causes people to seek the anonymity of the crowd, but in doing this, they often give up the close fellowship they actually seek.

More of the Same

As the local community church weakens and becomes ineffective, the membership begins to drift to other doors. Some of the cause of failure at the local level is burnout of faithful workers. This together with those too lazy to work creates an atmosphere for a "spectator" church rather than a church of participating worshipers. As these discouraged or disgruntled individuals drift into other assemblies, the leadership assumed they were attracted by their personalities and program; consequently, it is more of the same. Such an arrogant assumption could well be the seed from which a Growing Church develops.

Spectators lost in the Crowd

As a personality cult develops, the multitude grows sufficiently for the "spectators" to become lost in the crowd. Not wanting to give up the heritage of worship, they attend to satisfy their conscience and maintain a family tradition. If they enjoy the music, and the people appear friendly, attendance may be repeated week after week until discouragement rears its ugly head. This process continues until they are too pathetic to move on and simply attached themselves to a Growing Church for prestige, or other business reasons. At least they could slip in, sing a little, smile, and slip out without a full commitment. What the leadership of a Growing Church sees as corporate success, many are beginning to see as the seeds of failure for Christianity at a personal level.

LIVING ON REFLECTED LIGHT

Reflected light is called albedo. The moon has reflected light from the sun. Believers have reflected light from the Son of Righteousness and it should shine on the sinner's pathway to show them the way to God. But as blinded sheep many follow legalistic leaders, accept competing agendas, and allow opposing methodologies to replace the simple truth taught by parents and the church of their childhood. Without an internal redirection of the soul that regenerates the human spirit and reflects the Light of the Word, the world will remain in darkness. Without this "living by faith," little can be done to forestall the coming disaster for a Growing Church. Hiding behind the stained-glass windows and living on reflected light from ancient saints is a receipt for trouble ahead for any congregation.

PROGRESSIVE DEBAUCHERY

The church has been unable to reduce the negative effect of an intrusive multicultural society into the life-style of church members. Although most American Presidents have been identified with Christianity, the "bully pulpit" of the Presidency together with the combined pulpits of thousands of churches have been unable to stem the tide of moral decay and progressive debauchery in American life.

Clergy involvement in public life and political causes have not prevented discrimination or eliminated injustice in America.

MANY UNINTENTIONALLY HINDER

Drastic change is required to prepare Protestant Christianity for the "communications super-highway" and the certain cultural and technological changes in the future. A cultural framework for doctrine has created a brand name concept for Christianity. This development was based on the writings of past theologians and produced a freeze frame theology not relevant to the present generation. This, together with the mobility of society, has produced complex and confusing relationships within local congregations. Many unintentionally hinder the conversion of the next generation to the Christian Faith. To make Christianity viable in a multicultural society, there must be an internal redirection of the Protestant soul, which includes a return to a personal redeeming experience, moral accountability and daily commitment to a life-style that pleases God and reaches others with the good news of the Christian gospel.

Worship is a response to the "worth-ship" of God, not to the size of the congregation, the personality of the preacher, or the nature of the budget.

CHAPTER SIX

Settled Data from the Laws of Nature

PROJECT WAS STOPPED COLD

The question is not whether or not people should attempt to build a super-size Church? Surely it can be done when a group of determined people put their mind and money to the project. The primary question is should they attempt to build a larger than normal Church? Is it the best means of reaching the lost with the Gospel? Before the days of skyscrapers there were no tall buildings except the Tower of Babel and everyone knows what happened here. God stopped the project cold! Certainly, they could build a building that was high in the sky, but that was not God's plan for mankind. All the effort was not to be placed in one spot, but the whole known world needed to be populated and developed for the benefit of mankind.

The primary building material was wood and stone and this material was unable to support its own weight beyond the normal height of trees. Even structures of stone required support of wood and this further limited their ability to stand their own weight. In fact the tallest tree in the Redwood Forest is a little less than 400 feet and this is exceptional. Not until artificially developed building material; such as; steel and aluminum, were fabricated could contractors build taller structures. Nature has limits built into the molecular structure of all materials man uses to build buildings. What does this say about the human material used to build churches? Would anyone claim that church members today are better than the Believers of the House Churches of the New Testament? Can anyone find better discipleship? Can any local program match the one-year discipleship training program in Antioch (Acts 11) that turned eager to learn converts into Christ-like men?

Continued Growth is not Inherent in Nature

Continued growth is not inherent in nature or the social structure of society. In the wild, one does not normally discover a lion or zebra that has continued to grow much beyond the normal size of the group. Even among domesticated animals, cows in a herd are about the same size and chickens in the barnyard are relatively the same in size and weight. Trees in a forest normally have a fixed size for the area or region. All the corn growing in a field is about the same size and the seed, the soil, and the weather determine this size. A farmer can do little when defective seed, poor soil, or bad weather limits the crop. A similar process exists in the social organizations of human society and these processes are at work in the church whether or not they are recognized by the people involved.

LARGE GROWTH AN ABNORMALITY

Exceptional large growth is an abnormality at best and the result of unusual circumstances at the worst. Striving to be the biggest (1) it took 1,000 years and a unique watering system for the tree, (2) the process of gelding for the horse, (3) an overactive pituitary gland for the man, and (4) six tons of reinforced fiberglass for the cow. What will it take to be the largest Mega-Church in America? At what price? For what purpose?

(1) It took more than 1,000 years of incremental growth for the tallest living tree to reach 379 feet, 1 inch, or five stories higher than the Statue of Liberty. It is a Mendocino Tree, a coast redwood Sequoia, found at Montgomery State Reserve near Ukiah, California, USA. The tree was last measured in September 1998, with a diameter of 10 feet 4 inches. The Sequoia has a unique watering system that has assisted in sustaining its century of growth.

(2) The average American male is 5 ft 9.4 inches, but Robert Pershing Wadlow (1918 - 1940) was and is the tallest human being ever recorded. He reached 8' 11.1" inches height and 490 pounds in weight before his death at the age of 22. His height was due to an overactive pituitary gland.   Others will come to claim this title, but at what cost to their personal health?

(3) Since all cows are average, the Dairy Industry used six tons of reinforced fiberglass, to construct Salem Sue, the World's Largest "man-made" Cow standing 38 feet high. Sue was so big she had to be built in three sections to get her to the hill where she stands as a monument. There is no real Salem Sue! She is an advertising gimmick.

A TREE HAS SPECIFIC AREAS OF GROWTH

A tree grows in three specific aspects: (1) the roots (supply and nourishment system), (2) just beneath the bark (support structure system), and (3) at the terminal bud at the end of the limbs (foliage and fruit-bearing system). Unless all three of these areas grow and develop proportionally, the tree will not survive and produce fruit (seed) for reproduction. Those who plan and develop the structures of religious organizations could learn from the way a tree grows and develops.

There is a God- provided logical sequence and a proportional size for each aspect of growth. For example, a tree is normally as large in the deep underground supply and nourishment system as it is above ground in the visible part that is designed to bear foliage and seed-fruit. In other words, the root system that nourishes the life of the tree is about the same size as the branches and foliage. If the growth fails to be proportional, the structure becomes top heavy and first becomes limited fruit bearing, then subject to disease, and finally structure failure that brings disaster. What does this say for the top heavy, over visible super-Church that concentrates on the "show and tell" part, but neglects the deeper spiritual roots that are required for long term nourishment and viability?

In order to assure the proportionality of growth, there must be certain steps toward discipline and quality assurance. In the fruit-tree business this is called pruning. Although there is a negative aspect of pruning, the loss of some growth, the net results is more and a better quality fruit. The constant pruning of fruit trees keeps them within the natural size to receive nourishment from the root system. The church must be aware of the complications of size as it relates to fruit-bearing and viability. Could this be a reason smaller churches bear more fruit percentage wise than the larger ones?

Research has demonstrated the viability of the individual witness through a small congregation to produce converts when compared with the staff-oriented program of the larger churches. It is assumed that the problem of upward delegation occurs where the membership delegates by job description to paid staff the normal activities of outreach.

TREE GROWTH IS LIMITED BY NOURISHMENT

Nature nourishes trees with a supply of a watery liquid called sap. It moves upward in part through an intricate supply system with decreasing pressure. The taller a tree becomes the more difficult the natural nourishing becomes. Even a vacuum pump is limited to pulling water higher than about 36 feet. Sap-lifting forces created by evaporation and transpiration sustain trees that are taller than those adequately supplied with sap. This is a kind of breathing water through the leaves. In addition, adhesion and cohesion due to the stickiness of molecules in the fluid-carrying vessels nourish growth. It is complicated. The basic rise of the watery fluid is rapid; however, the other nourishing processes are much slower. In reality, the larger the tree the more difficult the nourishing process. This is especially true of fruit-bearing trees. The same is true of a church that is classified as God's Garden.

HOW DOES A GARDEN GROW?

A garden grows by diligent cultivation, careful prayerful planting, unceasing effort, constant attention, saintly patience, and then it must be touched by the Hand of God. Men alone do not build the church or the Kingdom. According to Paul we are co-laborers together with God, and together we are God's vineyard, God's Building. (1 Corinthians 3:9) We sow the seeds and water the plants, but it is God who gives the increase. (1 Corinthians 3:6, 7) Where are those willing to be seed sowers? Where are the water boys? Where are those willing to dung the fig tree? Where are those aware of the "no fruit" who is willing to petition God for one more year to work for productivity?

Surely God is working in the world to perfect the growth of His garden, but what about the part that was left for the human element. God provides the land, the sunshine, the rain, the minerals in the soil, but requires the farmer to cultivate, plant, continually watch, and wait for God to send the rain and sunshine. There is little that can be done without the Divine touch. Nature and the basic common experience of the human race inform the proper procedures to grow a garden.

Since the church is considered to be God's Garden, why then does it not grow properly? If one would study the Ceremonial Law, God gave the Hebrews, valuable lessons could be learned that might shed light on what God expects. (Leviticus 19 and Deuteronomy 22) "Thou shalt not sow thy field with mingled seed:"(Leviticus 19:19) "Thou shalt not sow thy vineyard with divers seeds: lest the fruit of thy seed which thou has sown, and the fruit of thy vineyard, be defiled." (Deuteronomy 22:9) The Hebrews were told not to plant two kinds of seeds in the same garden lest the fruit of the garden become defiled, because they did not yet understand cross-pollination. They were given specific guidelines to protect their crop from this mixture that created hybrids. The hybrid is a cross-breed and does not produce re-usable seed.

Modern agriculturist has refined the farming process so that one can plant and produce crops side by side by timing the planting. Could it be that churchmen have so manipulated the church-growing process that they are now producing a crop of hybrids? Could this mixture be an amalgamation that produces foundations and structures of iron and clay that will be destroyed by the "Rock coming down from the mountain" in the last days?

FOLIAGE BUT NO FRUIT

Size does affect fruit bearing, because a tree may utilize the nourishment available to grow leaves in an effort to appear viable and maybe catch a few more drops of rain. When there is nothing but leaves and the absence of expected fruit-bearing, the warning signs are visible, but no one seems to notice. As long as there is the appearance of life and some leaves from the "Garden of Eden" to cover the absence of full obedience, people translate the appearance into productivity and continue to support the top-heavy structure. There may be foliage, the appearance of life and the promise of fruit, but fruit is limited or missing altogether.

The ministry of Jesus clearly deals with this problem. The church must learn that leaves alone are not sufficient, to satisfy the Great Commission--there must be fruit. Remember the Gardner that petitioned Jesus for permission to work around the roots of a fruit-less tree? He wanted to put some fertilize around it and give it another year to produce fruit, but Jesus gave it only three years to produce fruit, then cursed the fig tree that had leaves but no fruit. What are the implications of this for the church? How long will good people tolerate the wasteful use of tithes and offerings to produce nothing but buildings, programs, staff, and more programs – only leaves that support the ego of a few but fails to bring fruit for the Kingdom?

LIMITS TO SIZE

In plant and animal life, there are limits to size. It has   been estimated that wood fiber could support the growth of a tree up to about 400 feet. The giant redwood trees of California stand high above all other trees on the planet, but they have not reached the limitation of 400 feet. The dinosaurs were of enormous size but they are now extinct. Speculation is that the climate changed and food became limited; consequently, the dinosaurs are gone and are relics of a bygone age. They are reconstructed now for museum presentation from fragments of bone. Scientist can determine from the size and structure of the skeletal remains the normal size of the animal. The limits of structure and environment are obvious and are applicable to human organizations as well as to both present and extinct plants and animals.

HEALTHY DEVELOPMENT

Organizational growth is not distinct; it follows the pattern of nature. Constructive coordination of differing facets into a complete and cohesive unit gives rise to healthy development in early rapid growth. Growth is not confined to the early stages, but the rate of growth is affected by the developmental phase in which the growth occurs. Some growth may continue as long as there is vitality, but mature growth has more to do with function than with size. The young may be evaluated based on size, but mature units are judged on the bases of quality.

CELL ENLARGEMENT AND CELL DUPLICATION

The normal growth of living things is perpetuated by cell enlargement and cell division, but the process does not always work effectively or efficiently. There is not always a readiness to grow or the resources to grow normally. In biology, one deals with the science of all forms of life, including their classification, physiology, chemistry, and interactions. This study is concerned with living organisms, their structure, function, growth, origin, abnormalities over time, and reproduction. Abnormalities include size, number, shape, color, and miscellaneous anomalies. The study of plant life includes vitality, survival, and reproductive strength.

In the study of Miller's Living Systems, all living things share commonalities of a specific origin, a pattern of developmental growth, viability, and decline and death. According to Miller, organisms, organizations, and institutions share a similar process. Since the church is considered a social institution, a local church or a collection of churches would share a similar life-span process. One thing is certain: the process of growth is dynamic and the phases or stages normally relate to the strengthening of the unit for viability and reproduction rather than being related to size.

ALL GROWTH IS TEMPORARY

The dynamic aspect of organizational growth and development goes through predictable stages. Failure to understand these phases locks the thinking of a congregation into fixed attitudes that handicap the effectiveness of the group function in the future.

All phases of growth are temporary; consequently, there is no continuous growth. This aspect of growth must be understood to avoid obstructions to development and adequacy. The constant effort to push quantity causes organized religion to neglect the quality needed to support and strengthen the basic fabric of Christianity.

ACCIDENTS WAITING TO HAPPEN

Many of the plans from the past and the organizations built on the reputation and good name of previous leaders are simply accidents waiting to happen. The structures of the past do not adequately inform the present. Even religious organizations are made of human design and limited by the human element.   Regardless of the spiritual nature of the enterprise, the human factor is still a liability.

JESUS CUT DOWN THE SIZE OF HIS CROWD

It is an amazing fact that some Church leaders feel they can minister to and shepherd thousands of members on the journey to spiritual fulfillment. Have they forgotten that Jesus Christ Himself consistently taught only twelve, that the congregations of Bible days were small house churches filled with the zeal and power of a first generation experience?   When one notes the facts related to the ministry of Jesus, they see a concern for quality not quantity. Jesus actually attempted to cut the size of His crowd down. He saw the crowd as following for the "loaves and fishes."

On one occasion, only three disciples remained and Jesus told them to go away, too. Peter declared, "Where are we going to go, you have the Words of Life;" consequently, the decision of Peter, James, and John to stay near to Christ was honored.   This was an effort to improve the quality and exactly the opposite of growth in numbers. When considering the quality of Christian commitment in the context of the Mega-Church, it is no wonder so many leaders fail to achieve their lofty goals.

Some years ago, my speaking at a Canadian Church Growth Conference created a discussion about the size of a church.   In reviewing my philosophy of growth, someone suggested that my view depreciated the large super-church in favor of the small community congregation. The question was asked "How large should a church be?" My response was, "How large should a cow be?" The questioner responded that he did not know. The group was asked if they were required to determine the normal size of a cow, how the process would work. It was suggested that perhaps one should observe and count some cows to determine the average or normal size. The apparent answer was that most mature cows were about the same size.

My next question was "What if you owned a cattle ranch and discovered a cow in the pasture that was 25 times larger than all the other cows, what would you do?" A participant answered, "I would get it out of the pasture as quickly as possible before it stepped on the other cows." The case is exactly the same for the super-church. If not in the process of becoming an abnormally large church, then soon after - other smaller congregations in the area would be trampled. This fact exists. Research demonstrated that in one southern city a large Baptist church had brought about the demise of thirteen other small Baptist churches. It is the law of the sea: big fish eat little fish. The application to congregation size was evident.

This is not to claim that a religious order or organization must lose the life and dynamics that nurtured it through periods of privation and persecution. When the changes that naturally occur in organizations are not understood, leaders are blind to the reality that organizations often deteriorate and fail in the fulfillment of their initial mission.

History indicates religious movements such as Judaism, Early Christianity, the Church of the Reformation, and many modern denominations began as vital, dynamic movements, but over time lapsed into cold, lifeless formalism as they matured into institutions. This does not mean that there was no life left in such an organization, it simply means that growth was limited to the resources and the environment in which an organization existed.

The super-church is too concerned about the facility, or the character of the architecture. What about outcomes in relation to mission? What about the quality of ministry in relation to service to a constituency? What about fruit bearing and harvest? What about a worthy contribution to society? What about genuine service to mankind? What about the non-quantitative "spiritual" aspects of the group?

To determine value or worth by numbers, whether people or dollars, is to devalue the worth of people. All growth is not good. The young are measured in terms of size and weight, but a mature adult would normally not be characterized in society by size. Of course, there are exceptions. Some athletes are identified by size and weight, but there are known health and social problems related to success in certain sports. The linebacker on the football team or a heavyweight champion boxer may have a few moments of glory, but these are short lived. Fame and health are here today and gone tomorrow. Aside from the monetary rewards, most healthy Americans would not wish to walk in their shoes or take the risks and punishment which characterizes these athletic achievements.

Unbridled or uncontrolled growth in humans is both malignant and destructive. Unlimited growth is abnormal and is characterized as a source of evil or anguish. Has the unlimited growth of the American government been good? Has the unlimited growth of one aspect of the economy not been harmful? Anti-trust laws protect trade and commerce from unlawful monopolies and unbridled growth of one sector of the economy. Christian congregations need to understand the risks of growth in quantity without improvement in the quality of the operation or service. When these factors: quantity and quality are balanced, the growth is normal and relates to the size of the population in the area.

Growth in size is good for the young, but for the mature, it is not growth in size that counts. It is development toward maturity and improvement in the quality of life and work. Why should a religious order or organization be judged by numerical size, the square feet of a building, or the number of people present on a specific occasion? To judge a small church based on size is to demean the sacrificial service of dedicated individuals who have unselfishly served others without asking for earthly reward. Also, to attribute value to the size of a super-sized church is to fail to see the complications of numbers.

Worship is a response to the "worth-ship" of God not to the size of the congregation, the personality of the preacher, or the nature of the budget. How much is God worth in the life of an individual or a congregation? This may not be measurable by scien-tific means, and may not be evident to the public, but it certainly exists. A Christian congregation should be evaluated on the bases of the quality of ministry and service to the community, not on attendance, baptisms or budgets. Without an emphasis on the qualitative aspects of organizational development, growth in numbers alone can become a liability to the Christianity community.

The future impact of Christian institutions on American life will depend more on the quality of the ministry to people and the nature of the services provided to the community than to meeting attendance or the size of the budget. Churches must avoid the Titanic blunder. The vision must be adjusted to include the raw material (people). The church can only build with people of faith. Trying to build on the Rock with hay and stubble will not stand the test of nature or time.

God never intended the collective light of believers to be used to advance a local ministry or impress a television audience.

CHAPTER SEVEN

Stern Counsel from the
S-Curve of Growth

GROWTH FOLLOWS THE PATTERN OF NATURE

Organizational growth is not distinct; it follows the pattern of nature. Constructive coordination of differing facets into a complete and cohesive unit gives rise to healthy development in early rapid growth. Growth is not confined to the early stages, but the rate of growth is affected by the developmental phase in which the growth occurs. Some growth may continue as long as there is vitality, but mature growth has more to do with function than with size. The young may be evaluated based on size, but mature units are judged on the bases of quality and performance. Productivity is the objective and to do this without loss or waste is the ideal.

GROWTH CONTINUES UNTIL THE
SATURATION BARRIER

An organism and an organization continue to grow through cell enlargement and cell duplication. This is part of the maturing and reproductive process and does not always work adequately. In fact, in Living Systems Theory the reproductive aspect of a "living system" is the only part of the process that does not have to work to remain viable. A state of growth exists in both an organism and an organization where the unit is alive and functioning, but does not reproduce itself.

The original unit itself may not continue to develop in size. Age retards the aspect of growth that contributes to size, but change continues to be present until death of the organism or the deterioration of the organization. Within this continuity, there are many metamorphosis-like critical periods of discontinued growth. It is during such phases that people get impatient and attempt to jump-start the process and end up producing something other than the original. One thing is certain: the process of growth is dynamic and the phases or stages normally relate to the strengthening of the unit rather than to the size. The phases when growth does not come naturally is the signal that strengthening what exist is the order of the day.

THE GROWTH CURVE

All growth follows the S-curve normally seen in plant and animal development; it is also evident in social organizations and institutions. The S-curve also exists in the life of human groups and organizations. The shape of the normal growth curve reveals a similarity between the growth curves of units and the whole. The growth of religious denominations and local congregations follows a similar curve. This growth curve has two opposing forces: a self-accelerating slope and a self-inhibiting slope. A constant rate of growth is normally observed until the targeted prospects disappear or the available resources both human and material are exhausted. Then following the use of all easily accessible resources, the growth-retarding factors initiate the declining slope.

An understanding of the S-curve of growth, that all living organisms and organizations exhibit is essential to comprehending the inner workings of an organization. The S-curve of growth (See Figure 7.1) has three phases: a period called the lag phase (I) when preparation is being made for growth. The period of actual growth called exponential or logarithmic phase (II). This period of rapid growth climaxed in maximum efficiency and usually gives way to a healthy development through a constructive coordination of differing facets of the organization into a uniform whole.

At this point in development, a stationary phase (III) usually develops because of the effort of the organization to survive. When the crisis is not met, the energies and resources normally used for outreach and expansion are re-channeled into the development of institutional design to maintain *status quo*; thus, the leveling off period is entered, when growth ceases and the size stabilizes. This is usually called the stationary phase or institutionalization phase and is most critical. It is critical because it is misunderstood. Most organizations and institutions reach this stage and maintain status quo for many years. Leadership should not become discouraged or impatient and attempt to jump-start the process. There is a simple process for rejuvenation, but it is painfully slow.

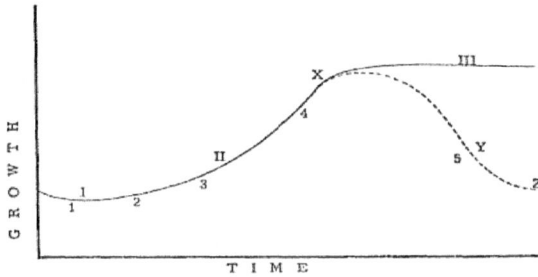

Figure 7.1 -- Diagram of the normal growth curve of an organization: I-lag phase, II-logarithmic phase, III-stationary phase, X-point of crisis. Y-decreased population. Z-fixed size below potential.

Sometimes in the standard development scheme of organizations the dynamic structure of growth is frustrated and the automatic nature of rejuvenation fails to work. The structures are modified progressively by processes operating within the organization as it evolves into a stable institution. Without understanding and patience, leaders can easily destroy the basic fabric of an organization and in fact create a new and different institution with a different mission. As painful as this may be, at times it is the only way an institution can survive with part of the early principles and goals intact.

Provided the organization survives, more formal rules are growth are properly supplied, expansion should continue until the growth curve (A-B) is repeated. The essentials of growth are: sufficient nutrients, energy in usable form, time, space, and the vitality of individual organisms. How does this translate to the present organization or institution? This is the real task of leadership increasingly imposed on the organizational constituency. This process produces a vicious cycle that impairs the effectiveness of the organization. The sociologists claim that if the organization survives the early developing years the constituency numbers normally increase and the property becomes more aesthetic. There are at least five anticipated states in this development that leadership must understand. (See Figure 7.2)

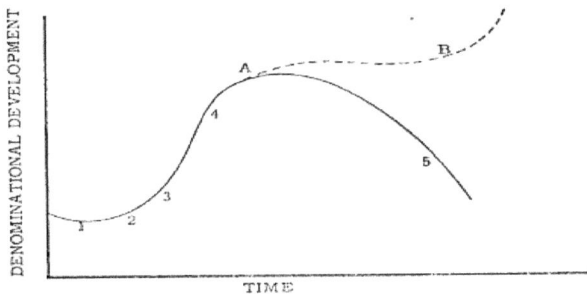

Figure 7.2 – Five stages of organizational development and these are numbered 1-5.

STAGES OF ORGANIZATIONAL DEVELOPMENT

The normal stages of organizational development are: (1) a weak association of individuals, (2) a formal organizational structure is established, (3) a period of maximum efficiency happens, (4) a more formal institutional stage becomes evident, and

(5) disintegration of the founding principles and constructs leads to decline or death. These stages seem to suggest an ultimate demoralization of all organizations; however, if at the crisis point (A) which comes early in the institutional stage, creative initiative is brought to bear on the problems and the essentials goals of the institution, acceptable progress can be made and the identity and integrity of the institution maintained.

Success normally contains the seeds of failure; consequently, growth itself creates a condition that may retard the process in accordance with the law of diminishing returns. The perpetual renewal of the whole structure is imperative to continue to support growth and development, but the tendency is for this renewal to be at an ever-decreasing rate. This is caused by the deterioration and hardening of the vital structures of growth. The slowing of the process with consequent increasing frequency of decay in various functions and facilities of either an organism or an organization reflects this loss of elasticity.

In examining the organizations of society, a distinct pattern emerges. Initial growth occurs as the carrying capacity of the social habitat is approached. The rate of growth decreases and normally leads to an organization of a fixed size. If the social habitat is destroyed, changed or drastically altered, the organization decreases in proportion to the decrease in the carrying capacity.

Notwithstanding the limitations of environment, provided an organization can adjust to the changing habitat it may survive, even stabilize and become fixed in size, but may be considerably smaller than its true potential had the resources and habitat been unlimited.   An example is the Swedish Baptist Church that began to die because the number of available Swedes declined. A name change and a mission to reach a larger population were effective in extending the life and effectiveness of the small denomination.

A look at the three main phases of a normal growth pattern makes the process of organizational growth easier to understand. There is a period of preparation for growth sometimes called the "lag phase." The time of actual growth is called the exponential or logarithmic phase and climaxes in maximum efficiency.   This phase usually gives way to healthy development. A constructive coordination of differing facets of the organization creates a uniform whole. When normal development has reached the extent of resources or environment, a stationary or institutional phase usually develops because of the efforts of the organization to survive.

The transition to the institutional phase is a turning point for the organization and can become a terminal phase for the institution. During this critical phase of development, the organization loses its flexibility and operations settle down to routine and often reactionary activities. This crisis is met by channeling the energies and resources previously used for growth and expansion into the creation of institutional structures designed to maintain the status quo.   Leaders began to concentrate on programs and projects that reflect their personalities and "simulate" progress.

This final phase is a leveling off period when growth ceases and the size stabilizes. In secular organizations this usually calls for mergers, name changes, diversification, or some campaign to influence the public that their product or service is new and improved and therefore better or best, or a least different and consequently better. The application to religious organizations or Christian congregations is apparent.

Developmental growth creates both formal and informal structures. The formal features of the organization are characterized by a command and task structure while friendship and interest dominate the informal aspects of the process. This structure is modified progressively by processes operating within the organization as it evolves into an institution. If the organization survives entrance into the institutional stage, formal rules are increasingly imposed upon members that are no longer a product of primarily voluntary interaction.

Rigid administration of both procedure and process tends to increase efficiency for a time, but ultimately, it produces a vicious cycle that impairs the effectiveness of the organization. Unless there is a relaxation of the formal aspects and an increase of the informal facets, the organization may collapse. In a best case scenario, the organization may find a size and continue for a time to be relatively effective with a limited audience.

Cooperation and interdependency are necessary in all areas of religious institutions. Growth in numbers, without consideration of the effect on quality, limits real progress in the development. In spite of the obstacles to quality, Christian congregations seem determined to increase size and budget without an adequate agenda for using either. This breeds unnecessary competition and personal strife among membership and frustrates the whole function of organization for the benefit of the people.

Perhaps a reminder that to serve an organization in administration is "to serve" the needs of the constituency, it does not mean, "to grow" unless the needs of present members can be met within the context of growth.   Since there seems to be no adequate way to measure quality of a religious organization, the process is surrogated to an assessment of religiosity.   This means counting noses and nickels and concentrating on budgets and buffets. Each organization can create its on criteria for being religious and project the belief that compliance with the formal aspects of this criteria makes one a better Christian than someone who is following another pattern of religious participation.

The anticipatory aspects of growth are often neglected. Growth causes an institution or organization to become more costly to operate and in the end less effective in many ways.   One distinguishing feature characterizing normal developmental growth is the anticipation of future needs, not only for the individual but also for the institution. When planning becomes limited, enough to cut off from view the long-ranged negative consequences of the growth; genuine progress has been drastically impeded.

In considering the Church as a "social institution,"
David O. Moberg determined five stages in the
growth and development of an organization.
The stages are (1) weak association, (2) formal
organization, (3) maximum efficiency (4) institutional
stage, and (5) disintegration. These steps seem to
suggest an ultimate demoralization of an organization
and the ultimate disintegration of an institution.
More than three decades ago, Findley B. Edge, in
his quest for vitality in religion wondered if the
tide of institutionalism could be stemmed and
the experiential, individual religious experience
be preserved within the context of American
Christianity. This question remains a perplexing
dilemma for which the American Church has found
no solution.

Growth will create change together with some
negative consequences. When a group accepts a
smaller number than the leader desires it affects
the positional ego and complicates the ministry of
presence required to produce effective leadership in
a religious organization. The alternatives are equally
undesirable; however, the size of a church should
be determined by the community not by the ego of
the minister. Many small community family-type
churches are doing effective work in reaching families
and serving communities. The big question "What is
the ideal size of a church congregation? Of course, it
depends on the nature of the community, but a rule
of thumb is somewhere between 40 and 300 people.
Only a few ministers can properly manage more
and normally the least talented can do well in the

smaller groups. God calls all kinds of ministers and the church should never put a God-called person in a place they are not able to handle.

The number 40 is used because that is the smallest number that creates the fellowship dynamics of a congregation with sufficient interpersonal relations so that everyone can find a friend. The Number 300 is used because God specifically determined, at least in the case of Gideon and Israel, anything over 300 was a problem for God getting the credit for ultimate victory over the enemy. Should we include women and children, the 300 could be stretched to nearly 1,000. Remember, the larger the group the more complicated the relationship and fellowship factors become.

~

What scripture called, "in the world, but not of the world" does not provide license for a dilatory attitude of noninvolvement.

CHAPTER EIGHT

Scattered Gleanings from the City-State

CITY-STATE CONCEPT

There are many similarities between the city-state system of Medieval History and the Mega-Church of the 21st Century. The city was the state and all those who lived under the protection of the city-state were citizens and owed unquestioned loyalty to the elders of the city. The elders sat in the main gate of the city and watched for strangers and foreigners. The people were citizens but had few rights or privileges.

Many constructs used by the church today originated with the city-state. The concept of the city-state in history informed how people and communities were understood. The city was walled for protection of those who lived within the gates, known as "citizens." It was walled to both keep the people in and strangers out. People who lived beyond the walls, on the heath (pastureland with low shrubs) were called "heathen", a loose rendering to the Latin for "pagan." Others who lived still farther beyond the heath in the woods or forest were known as "savages" or "forest dwellers." Travelers who passed the gates of the city were called "strangers and foreigners" and were mistrusted. Those who mounted armed assault against the city or simply harassed the citizens were known as "the enemy." When the strong men of the city went outside the protected sanctuary of the walls to drive off an enemy, they engaged in "warfare." One can easily see the connection between the city-state concept and the way the people of modern communities understand their life and circumstance. Casual observers of the church can see a few similarities related to the way churchmen see the community around them, the way evangelism and missions are constructed to reach the heathen and the savages.

A CULTURAL VIEW

The church sends missionaries to the heathen and the savages. Foreigners are still looked upon as being different, meaning "unlike us" or not as good as we are. Such attitudes breed false pride, bigotry, intolerance, discrimination, prejudice, and favoritism. Of course, this complicates any effort to unify the community for constructive progress or for the spiritual battles that must be fought to guard the faith and take back the moral high ground in the community.

The people who lived within the gates were called "citizens" and were under the authority and protection of the keepers of the gates and the selected assembly. If the keepers of the gates signaled all to assemble inside the city walls, the warriors then went to the walls to guard the people or resist the attacker.

It was a "one for all and all for one" attitude that clearly created an us-and-them mindset.

A Book of Cities

History primarily recorded data about towns and cities of significant size and importance. The New Testament was also a book of cities. Churches were established in the cities where the people lived and worked. The recorded mission and ministry of St. Paul was primarily a journey from Jerusalem the religious center to Rome the political center of the world of that day. No record exists of Paul working in small towns or rural communities. His mission was to take the message to the citizens of the cities and transform these citizens into viable spiritual communities. In fact, the churches in Paul's day were really a collection of believers from across a given community. There were no sectarian divisions. Historically, Paul seemed to be constantly on his way to Rome. Since the churches were established in the cities, it is easy to see how the early church translated the idea of good citizenship into the concept of moral and ethical living.

A One-Year Discipleship Project

When the early revival came to Antioch and Barnabas needed assistance in disciplining the new converts, Paul was invited to come to the city and assist with the teaching. The scripture was clear: a whole year they assembled themselves with the church, and taught much people. And the disciples were called Christians first in Antioch." (Acts 11.26) The converted "citizens," after a one-year

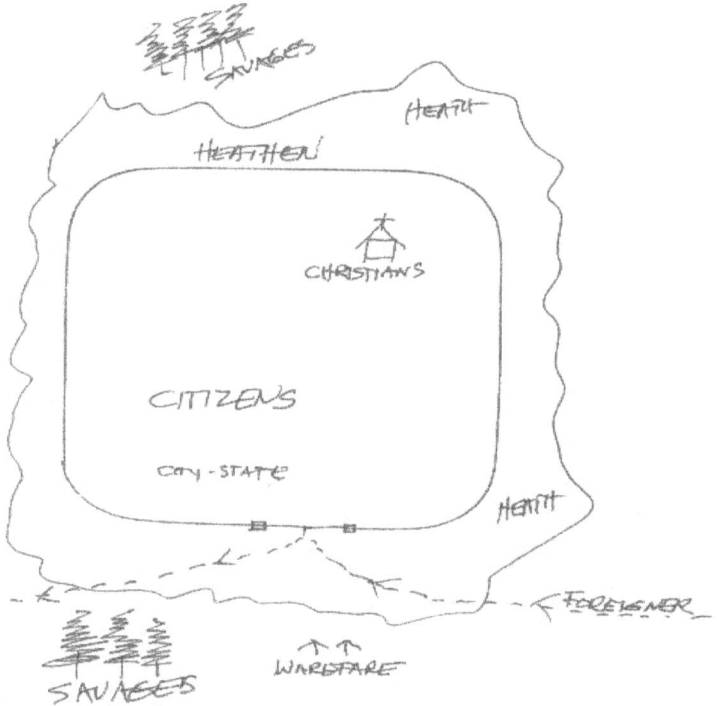

Figure 7.1 – City-State Cultural View

disciple-training program, became known as
"Christians." Yet these good folk brought with them
their culture, language, and baggage.

CITY-STATE LANGUAGE

Sadly the church eagerly added the rest of the
city-state language to their mission. The added
vocabulary included such words as heathen, savage,
foreigner, enemy, and warfare. What happened to
the special "citizen's council", *the called out ones*, who
functioned to equip and protect the community?

The Early Church used the same word, *ekklesia* to describe the mission of the church itself. The first converts were called out, equipped for ministry, and sent back into the community to minister to their own household and neighbors. This is where the early House Churches originated. Early Christians had both a spiritual and a political function in society. In some areas the church has all but abandoned their spiritual and political responsibility to the community.

A POLITICAL FUNCTION

The early Christians adopted a Greek word, *ekklesia*, for the church that had a political meaning. During the city-state era of Greek history *ekklesia* was used for the regularly summoned assembly of certain citizens charged with caring for the affairs of the city (state). At the cry of the Herald, the selected citizens would separate themselves from others and assemble at the meeting place ready to do the business of the community. Somewhere in the process of time, the church lost several aspects of the root meaning. This could be the primary cause for the lack of constructive social action in relation to the current breakdown of ethical and moral behavior.

AID AND COMFORT TO THE OPPOSITION

The selective nature of the called out ones has been abandoned. Masses of unredeemed and unholy people fill the churches. The "house of prayer" has truly been turned in to a den of thieves. The aspect of separation from worldly things to do special work has been minimized along with the idea of spiritual leadership roles that must function to protect the individual, the family, and the community. The community meetinghouses have been neglected and in some cases actually abandoned as discouraged and disgruntled members move on to become lost in the crowd of a Growing Church. The spiritual responsibility for others has been abdicated. The concern for the welfare of the "city" has been discarded for the spirit of laissez-faire (non-interference with the action of individuals). Such indifference becomes an aid and comfort to the enemies of all that is good and honest in the community and weakens the ability of moral leaders to defend the fortress of faith. What is a Growing Church doing for the common good of Christianity? Has it become a place of isolation and indifference to the needs of the community where they worship and let the world continue on the downward path to progressive debauchery?

The Common Good

All the essential elements of *ekklesia* were included in what the Greek version of the Old Testament called the assembly of Israel. The Septuagint used *ekklesia* to explain the essential function of the Jewish community. Another Greek word, *sunagoge* was used for the place of worship and instruction for the Jewish community. The concept of synagogue is to "bring or assemble together." The basic ideas of *ekklesia* and *sunagoge* were incorporated in the early gathering of believers and used as both a spiritual and political force in the community. Why does such opposition exist to people of faith gathering together

for the common good in each community? Why do
they abandon their own community and commute to
a "worship center" that cares little or nothing about
their home community?

A COMMUNITY OF KINDRED SOULS

Spiritual believers are not a colony of people on
a sojourn through a strange land who never become
part of the land. What scripture called, "in the world,
but not of the world" does not provide license for a
dilatory attitude of noninvolvement. A colony is a
group living in a location other than their homeland,
but remaining under the control of the home country
and maintaining all the customs and lifestyle of their
homeland. A modern community must be more than
a collection of people. A sense of community breeds
togetherness and cooperation for the common good.
True believers may feel that Heaven is their home,
but in the here and now they have responsibility
to be a active witness in the community. To be a
witness, requires a commitment to a lifestyle that
influences others to want to follow. Salvation in the
Christian sense separates one from sins not friends.
The salvation experience should motivate one toward
the saving of family and friends. It did in the New
Testament.

A GATHERING OF STRANGERS

St. Peter saw the early church "as strangers and
pilgrims" (1 Peter 2:11). Such citizens of the kingdom
living in a hostile world, gathered themselves in
congregations much like a fort and were bound
together similar to the rules that govern a community.

They were kindred minds joined in heart to bring
a constructive message and lifestyle to the new but
hostile land. The church is people not buildings. By
establishing religious buildings as compounds and
forts, the wrong message was sent to the world. The
church became something similar to a city-state entity
equipped both to protect the members and to carry
the good news to the population of the hostile land.

Finally, it deteriorated into a club for saints
and no one seems to care about the welfare of the
community. This "us-and-them" mentality has
diminished the value of the organized church in the
community. The mobility of the present society has
reinforced the church and community as a gathering
of strangers. Normally, a stranger is considered
neither a friend nor an acquaintance. What happed
to friendship evangelism? What happened to family
faith? What happened to concern for the neighbor's
soul? Must the congregation continue to sing and
worship in a stained-glass cathedral and continue to
close their eyes to the needs of lost family, neighbors,
and friends?

GROUP SPIRIT

The church cannot expect the existing system
of education or any other government program to
serve as an adequate catalyst for a moral renaissance.
Spiritual leaders, with contagious esprit de corps, are
required to effect moral change. Spiritual leadership
knows the church is the last line of defense for the
family, the community, and the cause of ethics and
morality in the nation. Somehow individual Believers
must recapture the excitement that existed in first

century Christianity. This excitement instituted an aggressive life-style evangelism that shared the good needs of the gospel everywhere they went.

MARTYRDOM

Among the early believers there was a defensive concern, aggressively displayed, for the corporate honor and interests of the group with particular concern for each member of the body. Each individual was willing to resist all evil even unto death for the cause. It is from this willingness to give life as a witness that we get the true understanding of martyrdom. Simon Peter's response to the betrayal of Jesus at Gethsemane was typical of the spirit of the early brotherhood.

When Judas came with a large company of religious leaders and elders of the city, Peter drew his sword and attacked. Out numbered, Peter went for a head and got an ear instead, but the spirit of resistance was there. This willingness of one sword against a mob typifies the aggressive nature of the early Christian witness. Martyrdom came about because an individual's lifestyle led to the risk of personal safety and security coupled ultimately with the willingness to give up life itself for the Cause.

The early Greek use of *martyr* and the present concept included in the word "witness" share the same root source and meaning. To affect renewal, the community must have committed individuals with a lifestyle that functions as an active witness in defense of morality and ethics. Such a willingness to confront contemporary culture when it violates

basic ethical and moral standards would identify the
areas of concern and bring public pressure to bear on
offensive conduct and produce constructive social
change.

~

CHAPTER NINE

Significant Lessons from Disaster

THE TITANIC BLUNDER

The desire to be the largest and best attended church in an area may weaken the effort toward excellence. Quality and quantity are mutually exclusive; increase one and decrease the other. There must be proportional balance between these two elements to maintain a viable state in any organization. When this is neglected or not understood, the results can be catastrophic. Striving to build the largest church in town or the effort of one local church to attempt to do all the ministries normally left to a denomination brings to mind the dreams of the builders of the Titanic.

EGO LARGER THAN TECHNOLOGY

Builders of the Titanic wanted to build the largest ship in the world. This was a noble goal, but their ego was larger than the shipbuilding technology of that day. Why did the Titanic sink? It hit an iceberg-- not really. It sank after it hit an iceberg. The Titanic sank because it was constructed with a quality of steel unable to withstand the cold. The water tight compartment doors did not close. The size of the ship also contributed to the break-up of the steel construction.

COMPETENT CREW NOT ENOUGH

It sank because the lookout in the crow's-nest was alert and signaled the bridge so the ship could turn in an effort to avoid the obstruction. The lookout was correct to warn the bridge. The crew was correct in turning sharply. However, had the ship rammed head-on into the iceberg it probably would have remained afloat or at least it would have taken longer to sink and many passengers would have been saved. By sideswiping the iceberg the hull was damaged, rivets popped, and the quality of steel was unable to withstand the pressure. It was not the extent of the damage, but the location that proved fatal.

The steel in the ship was brittle and could not absorb the massive amounts of pressure brought on by the water filled compartments. The ship literally broke apart. The real problem was the high sulfur content of the steel from which the ship was constructed. This made the steel fracture in the cold water under pressure. The steel makers used the best technology available and thought they had done a good job. They did not understand the concept of brittle fracture caused by high sulfur content in steel.

In reality, the shipbuilding design and technology was ahead of the knowledge of the steel makers. Those who made the steel were long dead before the technology was advanced sufficiently to explain the disaster. The steel with which the ship was built was not declared the reason for the disaster until eight decades after the ship went to the bottom of the sea.

The largest ship of the day, designed to be unsinkable- sank in less than three hours of hitting an iceberg. Some of the richest men in the world went down with the ship's captain and the architect who designed the unsinkable Titanic.   The sinking of the Titanic made changes in shipbuilding, the procedures for handling lifeboats, and in maritime communication. Yet, it was several generations before shipbuilding steel advanced sufficiently to meet the dreams of the architect or the maritime company.

SERIOUS GENERATIONAL CONCERNS

What concerns those who study church growth or the opposite (negative participation), is what will happen to the next generation? Will there be leaders of sufficient caliber to lead this group into the next generation? Will the false concepts and constructs learned by congregants of a super-size church surface and be corrected in time not to harm other congregations or the next generation? Remember when Paul engaged in a tent making business to relieve a local congregation of the support burden of his ministry? Later, Paul wrote this church and asked forgiveness for the "wrong," because they had not learned the lesson of responsibility to the leadership.

Will a growing Church staff do so much for the congregation that they will not learn the basic lessons of personal involvement and responsibility? Will it be a problem for the next generation? Will the seeds of failure spring up soon or be delayed for generations? These are important questions that no one has answered. No longitudinal study has been conducted to chart the patterns and develop an intervention procedure to reverse the trend. All that can be done is to look at history, Scripture, and human nature as predictors. When this is done, there is deep concern.

SMALL IS PART OF NATURE

Scripture is clear that one should never despise the day of small things. Remember the small church in a rural community when the congregation was a gathering of family and friends? In those days there was the family pew, the family altar, family prayer and daily devotions. Children were brought up in the fear and admonition of the Lord. Contrast that with the urban-church, the super-Church, the Mega-Church, the personality-led church, the dynasty-led church, or the stay at home-TV-church. Which one is preferred? Which one did the best job assisting parents in raising their children in a wholesome and moral environment? Which one ministered to the community, counseled, married, and buried the dead?

DREAMS OR VISIONS MAY NOT BE SUFFICIENT

The moral of the Titanic is that dreams or visions may not be enough. Well trained leaders and a competent crew may not be sufficient to meet a natural disaster when the construction of the ship is the problem. Could the mixture of transfer growth from several local churches and denominations ever construct a unified body of believers? Can an adequate church be built out of unconverted people? Could spectators in a super-Church ever become real participators in true worship? Can those who have been attracted to the church by entertainment become dependable members? Could those who desire to be "lost in the crowd" ever become personal one-on-one witnesses to the saving grace of Christ?

The big question: can the super-church be sustained over time? Will the same factors that caused the influx of transfer growth become a cause for a great exodus? When the disgruntled, discouraged, or disillusioned move from one church group to another they bring with them all the negative factors that precipitated the change in the first place. No longitudinal study has been made to understand this phenomenon. Will the lessons be learned in time to avoid disaster?

Observable facts seem to suggest that the danger of calamity appears certain. Impulsive individuals and people who constantly seek greener pastures usually move on at a hint of disagreement or a slight wind of change in discipline or practice. When the reason for wanting the change becomes obsolete, they will move again. In the midst of a different situation they often realize that the change was too drastic and wish to revert to the original state or search for another explorative move. As Jeremiah bluntly said to Israel: if you look to others for satisfaction you will find only misery because the problem is in you. "Why gaddest thou about so much to change thy way?"(Jeremiah2:36) One cannot move from a frustrating actuality into an all-satisfying reality when the real problem is personal.

One may not construct a superior until they correct the inferior. The Kingdom of God and the Christian movement would be much better if members would fix their personal problems and stay with their home church and work to reach their families and friends. The problems of life should be faced head-on and the consequences taken. Moving to a super-Church and becoming lost in the crowd does not advance the Cause. The move may appear to be a fix, but it is a temporary bandage for a festering wound. The place of worship is not the issue; it is the Person one wishes to worship.

PERSON INSTEAD OF PLACE

In the Old Testament the emphasis was on "place," the Tabernacle or the Synagogue as a place to worship, but in the New Testament the emphasis is on the Person of Jesus Christ. In the Old Testament the power and influence of a single Prophet or Judge was important, but throughout New Testament days the personality of the Apostles was not a consideration, only the Person of Jesus Christ was an object of worship. In the special consideration of grace there is no special place to worship or make a sacrifice of praise; wherever the individual Believer happens to be is an adequate place of worship.

Believers have a life-style and may worship anywhere at anytime without the assistance of programmed music or the sway of a worship leader. What counts is the attitude of the heart and one's relationship to Jesus Christ that produces a life-style of daily sharing the faith. As converts are multiplied into a redeeming Body scattered throughout the community, God's saving grace is extended. Has a Growing Church caused believers to become too attached and obligated to a special place instead of developing a daily life-style pleasing to God? Is the Scriptural mandate being ignored?

CONCLUSION

It is not sufficient to have a good idea; one must understand the consequences of the idea. Even doing one's job well is not enough to avert human disaster. The steel makers, the ship builders, or even the alertness of the lookout in the crow's nest or the quick and proper response of the crew on the bridge could not make the difference in the design or the faulty material with which the architect's dream boat was constructed. Usually, attempts to avert disaster fail because of previous errors in judgment. An old saying rings true, "the bigger they are the harder they fall." What implications does this have for a growing church?

The striving to build the largest church in town or the effort of one local church to attempt all the ministry normally left to an organized group of churches, brings to mind the dreams of the Titanic builders. A major lesson we can learn from the Titanic is that dreams may not be sufficient to construct a long term solution to Christian watch-care.